The Prayer Jar

DEVOTIONAL

HOPE

The Prayer Jar

DEVOTIONAL

HOPE

WANDA E.
BRUNSTETTER

with

DONNA K. MALTESE

BARBOUR

PUBLISHING

HOPE

According to Webster's Dictionary, the word *hope* means "desire with expectation of obtaining what is desired, or belief that it is obtainable." The Bible's definition of hope is "the anticipation of a favorable outcome under God's guidance."

If ever there was a time that our world needs hope, it's now. Some people sink into depression when they feel there is no hope; others turn to alcohol, drugs, and other addictions. The truth is, without Christ, there is no hope. That is why those who are Christians can feel hopeful even during the most unsettling circumstances.

We have hope because we have faith in a trustworthy God. People who've placed their hope in someone or something other than Jesus are often disappointed. The Lord wants us to live each day with spiritual and emotional anticipation that a favorable outcome is in our future. We are to remind ourselves of the promises of God—and trust in the One who is faithful in keeping His promises.

It is my prayer that each person who reads this devotional will find within its pages the true hope that comes from having a personal relationship with God's one and only Son, Jesus—the Savior of the world. Every believer can have hope for the future, a renewed faith in God, and the assurance that He is always with us. It's because of Him that we can always have hope.

Let thy mercy, O Lord, be upon us,
according as we hope in thee.

Psalm 33:22 kjv

WHAT IS A PRAYER JAR?

One of the most important things we can do to keep hope alive is pray. The Bible tells us in James 4:8 that if we want to draw closer to God, we are to reach out to Him. By going to God in prayer, we are able to offer our adoration, petitions, intercession, and thanks to Him. One thing we can do to remind ourselves to pray often is make a prayer jar and place it where we will see it every day. Each time we look at the jar, we will think of who and what we want to pray for. A prayer jar can deepen our relationship with God and strengthen our faith.

A prayer jar can be something as simple as a canning jar. It can be left plain or decorated with ribbon, stickers, buttons, sequins, feathers, or glitter. The one I use is an antique canning jar, which I've left plain. I write my prayer requests, verses of scripture, or notes of thanks to God on small pieces of paper. After praying about the request or reflecting on the Bible verse, I fold the paper in half and place it in the prayer jar. From time to time, I take out one or more of the prayers—and if that particular prayer has been answered, I thank the Lord for answered prayer and then write down the date. If my prayer request has not yet been answered, it goes back into the jar. Do you have a special prayer request today? If so, consider creating your own prayer jar.

HOPE
for Strength

Have you ever felt so weak, physically or emotionally, that you thought you couldn't go on? In your own strength, did you try to keep forging ahead, or did you take time to pray about it? If you're like me, you sometimes try to do things in your own strength, hoping everything will turn out as it should. But hoping for strength isn't enough. As Christians, we need to rely on God's power to strengthen and help us with all the challenges we face. Isaiah 40:31 (KJV) is a good verse to focus on during times when you feel that your strength is gone: "But they that wait upon the LORD shall renew their strength; they shall mount up with wings as eagles; they shall run, and not be weary; and they shall walk, and not faint."

My greatest times of growth have been when I reached the end of my resources and realized that all I had left was Jesus. God uses suffering and our weaknesses to make us rely on Him. His grace is sufficient even when we feel weak, and during such times, God can make us stronger than we have ever been.

Aren't you glad that whenever we face trials in this life, God is with us and He renews our strength and faith? "Be of good courage, and he shall strengthen your heart, all ye that hope in the LORD" (Psalm 31:24 KJV).

RENEWABLE STRENGTH

*Those who trust in the Lord will renew their strength;
they will soar on wings like eagles; they will run and
not grow weary; they will walk and not faint.*

ISAIAH 40:31 HCSB

The alarm goes off. Still heavy with sleep, you reluctantly pull your arm out from underneath the covers and hit the SNOOZE button. *Just one more minute,* you think to yourself, *and then I'll get up. Perhaps then I'll have the energy to face this day.*

Those kinds of thoughts speak to the spirit of women who aren't necessarily morning people. We wonder how and where we're going to get the strength to accomplish all the things we want or need to do today.

Yet God has another message He'd like you to engrave on your mind. And that's the hope that *He* will give you all the strength you need to get through your day. Only one ingredient is necessary: your trust in Him.

Each day, ask God what He would have you do. And He will give you the energy to do it. How is this possible? Well, He's God. "He never grows faint or weary" (Isaiah 40:28 HCSB).

*Lord, I hope in Your strength, knowing You will give me the
energy to do what You would have me do today. Amen.*

PRAYER JAR INSPIRATION:

God will renew my strength each day.

PERSONALLY AHEAD

"So be strong and courageous! Do not be afraid and do not panic before them. For the Lᴏʀᴅ your God will personally go ahead of you. He will neither fail you nor abandon you."

Dᴇᴜᴛᴇʀᴏɴᴏᴍʏ 31:6 ɴʟᴛ

The world can be a very scary place. We never know what might be waiting for us around the next corner, the next bend in the road. And overloading ourselves on news about wars, viruses, random shootings, and such makes us even more anxious and fearful. Yet that is *not* what God wants for us.

Moses had gotten God's people as far as the Jordan River. And just beyond that river was the Promised Land. From that moment on, Joshua would have to lead God's people. So, in his farewell address to the Israelites, Moses told them that they could be strong and brave. They need not panic nor be afraid—because God Himself was going ahead of them. He would always be there for them.

The same holds true for you. You are one of God's followers. So put all panic, fear, and weakness behind you. Instead, walk in the hope that God is going ahead of you personally. And always will.

Thank You, Lord, for giving me the strength and courage to go on, to go where You lead. Amen.

PRAYER JAR INSPIRATION:

God, lead the way in Your strength.

CALLED FOR

On the day I called, You answered me; and You made me
bold and confident with [renewed] strength in my life.

PSALM 138:3 AMP

Day after day goes by, and still you cannot seem to find the strength to do what your heart truly desires: to fulfill the plans God has set before you. What's a woman to do?

Pray. Go to God. Sit, kneel, prostrate yourself before Him. Push from your mind all the ifs, ands, or buts that stand between you and the goals God has planted in your heart. Allow yourself to be filled with the Spirit's presence. Focus on your breath, allowing it to match the endless rhythm of God's heartbeat. And when you sense God within and without, call on Him. Make your request known. If you cannot put it into words, present your groans and moans, knowing the Spirit will translate your petition, knowing that God will answer your request or change it so that your desire matches His will.

Ask God to give you the courage and strength you need to do what He has called you to do—no matter how impossible or improbable it may seem. Then rise up, filled with the hope and certainty that what God deems to be will become your reality.

Lord, I call on You for strength to realize my dream.

PRAYER JAR INSPIRATION:

God of all living, renew my strength; embolden my heart.

ALWAYS FOUND

God is our refuge and strength, a helper who is always found
in times of trouble. Therefore we will not be afraid.

Psalm 46:1–2 hcsb

The world is constantly changing. Things we never imagined would ever happen are becoming the norm—especially the unpredictable weather. Because of climate change, we're seeing extreme weather patterns raging all around us.

Fortunately, we have God in our lives. We have a Savior, an eternal Helper, who has proved in the past and the present that He's always there for us. In Him, we can put all our hope and find our refuge and strength amid troubled times. "Therefore we will not be afraid, though the earth trembles and the mountains topple into the depths of the seas, though its waters roar and foam and the mountains quake with its turmoil" (Psalm 46:2–3 hcsb).

Woman of God, you never need to fear or feel too weak to find your footing in the flood or to secure a safe place behind the flames of fire. God will always be there for you to give you strength.

Holy Refuge and Strength, thank You for always being there
when trouble comes. Because of Your constant presence amid
flood, wind, and fire, I will find the strength when I need it.

PRAYER JAR INSPIRATION:

God of strength, be my constant Refuge in
this time. Help me keep my eyes on You.

REMADE

*After you have suffered for a little while, the God of all grace
[who imparts His blessing and favor], who called you to His own
eternal glory in Christ, will Himself complete, confirm, strengthen,
and establish you [making you what you ought to be].*

1 Peter 5:10 AMP

Life can be difficult. But even though you may experience some suffering now and then, you are not to lose hope. Instead, remember that the Lord of all creation—the One who fashioned you for a special purpose that only *you* can live out—may allow some trouble to come your way so that you become the woman He created you to be. It's true! God will use those difficulties to strengthen you, to transform you into the precious daughter *He already considers you to be.*

When God saw Gideon cowering in a corner, He addressed him as a mighty warrior! How could this man in hiding—the one whose family was the weakest in his tribe and who was the youngest in his family—be a warrior? By going in the strength he had, knowing God was with him (Judges 6:11–14).

So, woman of God, go in the strength you have. Be the woman the Lord already knows you are. And do so without fear, knowing He goes with you.

Thank You, Lord, for making me complete in Your eyes.

PRAYER JAR INSPIRATION:

God remakes me in His strength and presence.

FALSE HOPE

A king is not saved by a large army; a warrior will not
be delivered by great strength. The horse is a false hope
for safety; it provides no escape by its great power.

PSALM 33:16–17 HCSB

When you find yourself in trouble, you might look to friends and family for strength and power. You may even look to money or possessions to help you escape the evil that is coming your way.

Yet other people—no matter how much they love you or how much wisdom they possess—cannot deliver you. Neither can money or possessions. But God—the One before whom the entire earth trembles, the One who parted seas and made the earth open up—can save you. For the Lord is the One who "spoke, and it [the world] came into being; He commanded, and it came into existence" (Psalm 33:9 HCSB).

If you are looking to be saved, to get yourself out of an impossible situation, turn to God. He is the One who has the strength to save you. He is the One who rules all peoples and all nature. He is the One who will remove the mountain of obstacles standing in your way and the evils barreling toward you. Put your hope in Him, the One who is never false.

Save me, Lord, by Your great strength.

PRAYER JAR INSPIRATION:

God, the All-Powerful, is my only true hope.
I entrust myself and all that I am to Him.

PEP TALK

"No man will [be able to] stand before you [to oppose you] as long as you live. Just as I was [present] with Moses, so will I be with you; I will not fail you or abandon you. Be strong and confident and courageous."

JOSHUA 1:5–6 AMP

After Moses died, God gave Joshua a good pep talk. He told him that just as He had been with Moses—guiding him, giving him encouragement and strength—He would be with Joshua. He would never fail him nor leave him. It was these words that gave Joshua the power to go on with the grand plan God had outlined for him as an individual and for the people he would lead.

God has a grand plan for you as well. And even though you may at times feel alone on the road He has set before you, He is walking right beside you. He will neither fail nor abandon you. Knowing that will give you all the strength, confidence, and courage you need to see things through.

Thank You, Lord, for this pep talk. I needed it so much right now. Knowing that You are walking at my side and will never abandon me gives me the strength and courage to do whatever You would have me do. In Jesus' name. Amen.

PRAYER JAR INSPIRATION:

God forever walks by my side, enabling me to do what He has called me to do.

A STRONG TOWER

The name of the LORD is a strong tower; the righteous
runs to it and is safe and set on high [far above evil].

PROVERBS 18:10 AMP

When the world is crumbling down around you, when the load on you is so heavy you can barely breathe, when you are feeling weaker than weak, there is a place you can go. To Yahweh, the Lord. His name is a strong tower. You can run to Him and find safety from all that bedevils and bewilders you. In His name, you can rise above every evil that threatens you. As you look down from His tower, all the troubles of this world become mere flotsam floating by, drifting way below you and out to an endless sea.

For the Lord's name is faithfulness, power, mercy, compassion, love, protection, safety, grace, goodness, and wisdom. All those things—all that He is—surround you when you reside in the tower of His strength.

So the next time troubles tap on your door or worries threaten to wound you, run to the name of the Lord. Shut the door behind you. And allow Him to renew you, to replenish your strength, to shield you from what threatens to harm you. In Him, you are safe.

Lord, my Mercy and Strength, to You I run.

PRAYER JAR INSPIRATION:

I find hope, shelter, and strength in the name of my Lord.

A DIFFERENT TUNE

*"The LORD is my strength and my song; he has given me victory.
This is my God, and I will praise him—my father's God, and I
will exalt him! The LORD is a warrior; Yahweh is his name!"*

EXODUS 15:2–3 NLT

Trouble is a relative term. To some it can mean a broken fingernail that snags some yarn while knitting. To others it can mean losing a job and not being able to pay the mortgage, or being ill and not having a way to get to the doctor, or being asked for a divorce just after moving to a new town, or being diagnosed with breast cancer and waiting to hear your options, or having a tree fall on your house just when you've finished remodeling the kitchen.

Yet none of those scenarios seem as troublesome as when the Israelites found themselves standing between an Egyptian army and the Red Sea. But God brought them out of that predicament. He did the impossible, parting the waters so His people could cross on dry land. Then He brought the waters back so their enemy would drown and never be seen again!

When you find yourself between a rock and a hard place, remember your Strength and Song. Call on God's power. And you'll find yourself singing a different tune in no time!

Help me, Lord! Give me strength amid trouble!

PRAYER JAR INSPIRATION:

God will change my song of pain to one of praise!

CONTINUALLY LOOKING

Search for the LORD and for his strength; continually seek him.
Remember the wonders he has performed. . . . Honor and
majesty surround him; strength and joy fill his dwelling.

1 CHRONICLES 16:11–12, 27 NLT

Every day a woman has her full list of chores before her—if not on paper then on the screen of her mind. With such a long list of have-to-dos or want-to-dos, she can easily get caught up in the busyness of her day and rarely take a moment to think about God, maybe forgetting Him entirely. Before she knows it, the sun has set, and she's too weak to do anything but flop into bed.

Yet that's not what God has envisioned for His Eves. He wants them to be continually looking for His presence and His strength. To be seeking Him every moment of every day. God wants His daughters to remind themselves of the wonders He has done and is doing and will do in the future. For only in the Lord will His girls find all the strength and joy they hope for at the beginning, middle, and end of each day.

Help me, Lord, to keep my mind and eyes
looking for You in every moment of my day.

PRAYER JAR INSPIRATION:

I'll be looking for You, Lord, around every corner!

STRENGTH IN WEAKNESS

He has said to me, "My grace is sufficient for you [My lovingkindness and My mercy are more than enough—always available—regardless of the situation]; for [My] power is being perfected [and is completed and shows itself most effectively] in [your] weakness." Therefore, I will all the more gladly boast in my weaknesses, so that the power of Christ [may completely enfold me and] may dwell in me.

2 Corinthians 12:9 AMP

What do you do with your hope when you've prayed and prayed and prayed and still gotten no relief from God for your physical, mental, or emotional trouble? Do you give up on Him, or do you turn to Him even more?

The apostle Paul had a "thorn in the flesh" (2 Corinthians 12:7) that tormented him. Three times he asked the Lord to take it away from him. But Jesus told him that His grace, His abundant and continual supply of love and mercy, was enough to carry Paul through his trouble. That *His* strength and power were going to work best through Paul's weakness.

So, don't lean into the enemy's whispers that God has abandoned you. Instead, tap into the abundant grace and power that Christ is pouring into you. Then you too will find the joy of Christ's strength dwelling in and enfolding you even in moments of weakness.

Enfold me, Lord, in Your power and strength.

PRAYER JAR INSPIRATION:

My hope in Christ lives on!

GOOD THINGS TO COME

*"The grass withers and the flowers fade,
but the word of our God stands forever."*

Isaiah 40:8 nlt

The things of this world are always changing. Every year, the grass turns brown and the flowers shrivel. The leaves fall and the trees stand bare. The butterflies and birds find other places to display their beauty. The snow comes, transforming the world into a white wonderland. Then just when you cannot take another day of ice and frigid winds, the crocuses begin to pop up, displaying their beauty once more. Upon seeing them, your hope of new things to come bursts through your winter doldrums, just as it did the year before.

Yes, much in this world is changeable. There's not much you can count on, as nothing remains the same. Except for God. And His Word. They never change. And because they never change, you can find your rock-solid strength in both.

Today, sink your mind into God's Word. Let Him and His promises give you the strength you need to love as He loves, to live as He would have you live—in the hope that good things are within your reach, with even more to come.

*Thank You, Lord, for the strength I find in
Your eternal presence and Word. Amen.*

PRAYER JAR INSPIRATION:

In God's never-changing Word, I find my hope and strength.

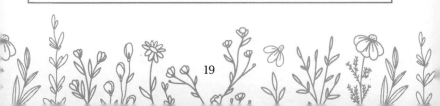

ENCIRCLED WITH STRENGTH

The God who encircles me with strength and makes my way blameless?
He makes my feet like hinds' feet [able to stand firmly and tread safely on
paths of testing and trouble]; He sets me [securely] upon my high places.

PSALM 18:32–33 AMP

Society may consider you, as a female, to be a member of the weaker sex. But in God's eyes you are anything but weak. Why? Because it is God, the One who created and sustains the planet you're standing on, who encircles you with His strength. It is God who aims you in the right direction so that you won't run afoul of any evil.

And it is this same Lord of lords who helps you so that you can have a firm footing. You can walk safely on life's roadway of challenges and troubles. With God in your life, you can stand strong on the highest of heights!

Today, remember in whom all your hopes lie. Feel the Lord's power encircling your entire being—mind, body, spirit, and soul. Get it into your head that He not only shields you but gives you the energy and power to do all you need to do. Who knows how high you will grow!

Encircle me with Your strength, Lord,
and my feet will stay steady on Your path.

PRAYER JAR INSPIRATION:

God encircles my entire being with His strength!

TREASURED BY GOD

"How can someone like me, your servant, speak with someone like you, my lord? Now I have no strength, and there is no breath in me." . . . He said, "Don't be afraid, you who are treasured by God. Peace to you; be very strong!" As he spoke to me, I was strengthened.

DANIEL 10:17, 19 HCSB

When the angel Gabriel came to reveal some things to Daniel, the latter was overwhelmed by what was happening. Who was he that he should be told these visions and learn what God was going to do?

God reveals much to those who are humble, faithful, and praying followers of Him. For they are part of His plan. They have a role to play. And when those who are loved by the Lord feel weak, God sends a divine word to boost their strength and calm their hearts.

God has a plan for you. To work out that plan, you must realize who you are: a person loved and treasured by God. And if at any time you go weak in the knees when thinking about or playing your part, turn to God. Tell Him how you're feeling. Know that He will give you all the attention, love, peace, and strength you need to live out His Word for you.

Thank You, Lord, for Your words of peace and strength.

PRAYER JAR INSPIRATION:

Treasured by God, I receive His peace and strength.

ULTIMATE PROVIDER

Riches and honor come from You, and You are the ruler of everything. Power and might are in Your hand, and it is in Your hand to make great and to give strength to all. Now therefore, our God, we give You thanks and praise Your glorious name.

1 Chronicles 29:12–13 HCSB

Everything we have comes from God. Not one thing is our own creation. He is the true source of all we desire, all we need. Yet how often do we give Him the thanks He deserves? How much of His bounty do we take for granted?

Today, remember that God is your ultimate and abundant Creator and Provider of everything you desire and need to live, to breathe, and to walk His Way. Get down on your knees and thank Him for the hope and strength He equips and inspires you with. Then use those blessings to live out His plan for you. Dream with the ultimate dreamer. Walk in step with the grand planner. And you will find all you need and hope for.

Everything I am and have, Lord, has come from Your loving hand. For this I thank, honor, and worship You. Help me use Your blessings to further Your kingdom. In Jesus' name.

PRAYER JAR INSPIRATION:

My hope and strength are gifts from my Lord. To Him I give all my thanks.

MOUNTAIN-MOVING MAMA

*"I assure you and most solemnly say to you, if you have
[living] faith the size of a mustard seed, you will say to this
mountain, 'Move from here to there,' and [if it is God's will]
it will move; and nothing will be impossible for you."*

MATTHEW 17:20 AMP

Some days you may feel as if everything is against you—as if all you
do is spend your time trying to overcome one obstacle after another.
At the end of the day, you feel not only weak and exhausted but a bit
disgusted with yourself and the world.

That's when you need to remember the power that is yours if you
will only take it and go deep. Jesus promises that with even the littlest
bit of trust and confidence in Him, you can say to any mountainous
obstacle you face, "Get out of my way," and if God wills it, it will
disintegrate. Whenever you dig deep in your faith, nothing will be
impossible for you. You'll be God's mountain-moving mama!

*Lord, when I feel weak, when I can no longer overcome the obstacles
before me, please remind me that I can move mountains. That with
You in my life, nothing will be impossible for me. In Your name, amen.*

PRAYER JAR INSPIRATION:

*With Jesus by my side, I hang on to the hope
that I can and will do the impossible.*

ALL YOU NEED

My God in His [steadfast] lovingkindness will meet me. . . .
I will sing of Your mighty strength and power; yes, I will sing
joyfully of Your lovingkindness in the morning; for You have
been my stronghold and a refuge in the day of my distress.

PSALM 59:10, 16 AMP

Before you even know what you need, your loving God has His ample supply of provisions ready to meet you. That's because He sees everything that's going on in your life. He knows all your thoughts, your feelings, your dreams, your hopes, and your requirements. And He knows exactly what you will encounter every day, way before you have an inkling of what's ahead.

So don't just hope that God will be there with His strength, love, and courage when you need it. *Know* He will be there with whatever you need so you do what you need to do for Him. Then afterward, sing joyfully of His love, His kindness, His strength, His protection, and His provision, knowing all He has for you will always be there for the asking and the taking.

Thank You, Lord, for having all I need just when I need it!

PRAYER JAR INSPIRATION:

Each day, I hope for and will sing of God's endless
blessings ready and waiting just for me.

YOUR ARM

O Lord, be gracious to us; we have waited [expectantly] for You.
Be the arm of Your servants every morning [that is, their strength
and their defense], our salvation also in the time of trouble.

Isaiah 33:2 AMP

You're sitting down to breakfast with eyes yearning to close. You reach for your coffee and take a sip, hoping it will give you the energy you need to shower and dress and then begin what you imagine will be a long, arduous day.

It's time to change that already-defeated mindset and attitude!

Remember who you are: a woman warrior. You are a follower of the all-powerful Creator God. Knowing He's on your side, allow Him to do what He is prepared to do: be your arm, your strength, every morning. One who will not only fight for you but defend you. And in case there happens to be some trouble coming your way, He will be there to rescue you.

Before your feet hit the floor in the morning, lift up your arms as if you were going to lift a heavy weight. Say to God, "Lord, be my arm every morning." Then move your forearms in front of your face and say, "Be my Strength and Defense." Then, and only then, arise and face your day!

Lord, be my arm—my Strength and Defense!

PRAYER JAR INSPIRATION:

God's strength and protection await me each day!

STANDING BY

At my first trial no one supported me [as an advocate] or stood with me,
but they all deserted me. May it not be counted against them [by God].
But the Lord stood by me and strengthened and empowered me, so that
through me the [gospel] message might be fully proclaimed, and that all
the Gentiles might hear it; and I was rescued from the mouth of the lion.

2 TIMOTHY 4:16–17 AMP

When Paul stood before the Roman tribunal, facing a death sentence, all his friends and coworkers deserted him. But the Lord didn't. He not only stood by Paul but gave him divine strength and power so that he could escape being beaten by those who stood against him.

If at any point you are in dire need of support or some sort of defense, take heart. Remember that just as the Lord stood by Paul, He stands by you. He is the best and greatest Defense and Strengthener you could ever ask for. He'll make sure that when all is said and done, you, like Daniel, have not one mark of a lion's tooth or claw on you (Daniel 6:23).

Thank You, Lord, for being the one Support
and Strengthener I can truly count on.

PRAYER JAR INSPIRATION:

I live in the hope and knowledge that God stands beside me,
giving me the strength and power I need to do His will.

HOPE
for Love

From the time we are born, we need love. A baby who doesn't receive love and nurturing will not survive. When you are shown love, you believe in what you can be. You become hopeful that there is still good in this world, and you learn to love yourself. When you share love with others, it begins the cycle over again. In 1 Corinthians 13:13 (NIV) it says, "And now these three remain: faith, hope and love. But the greatest of these is love."

Hebrews 11:1 (NIV) gives us a clear definition of faith: "Now faith is confidence in what we hope for and assurance about what we do not see." Faith is the belief that there's something better to seek; hope is the expectation that it is there. Hope is the fuel that keeps faith alive in our pursuit of love. Love is the result that we see of our faith and hope.

First John 4:19 (NIV) states: "We love because he first loved us." Believers in Christ should make love a priority, as we are told in John 13:34 (NIV): "A new command I give you: Love one another. As I have loved you, so you must love one another." When we demonstrate Christian love, it distinguishes believers from the rest of the world. Love opens up its life to another person and goes beyond sentimental feelings. It breaks down barriers and exposes our hearts.

GOD IS LOVE

*God is love. . . . And we have come to know and to believe
the love that God has for us. God is love, and the one who
remains in love remains in God, and God remains in him.*

1 JOHN 4:8, 16 HCSB

Here we have a few very powerful and amazing truths. The first is
that God is love. The second is that He has an amazing amount of
love for us.

Yet that's not all! John tells us that because God is love, the woman
who abides in love, who lives it out in her life, abides in God—and
God abides in her! Consider that idea, that fact. The Creator and
Sustainer of the entire planet, solar system, and universe—the One
who holds all the power and people of this earth in His hand—this
God, this Person, this Spirit is love. And if we dwell in that love, not
only do we live in Him, but He lives in us!

In those moments when you feel unlovable, unloved, and unable
to love, remember the hope you have in the God who is love. And
soon you will find yourself overwhelmed by His love.

Thank You, Lord, for allowing me to experience Your love.

PRAYER JAR INSPIRATION:

I hope in the God of love.

CONSTANT LOVE

He heals the brokenhearted and binds up their
wounds. . . . The Lord takes pleasure in those who
fear him, in those who hope in his steadfast love.

PSALM 147:3, 11 ESV

We all have those days when we feel as if no one loves us. . .when disappointment after disappointment cracks our foundation of strength. . . when we feel exhausted, as if we have been trying in vain to swim against a strong current. . .when absolutely nothing is going our way.

Buck up, woman! Take heart in the fact that God loves you. He is cognizant of all that is going on in your life. He gathers to Him those cast out. He heals those with broken hearts. He binds up the wounds of those crushed in spirit and lifts those who are humble.

It's okay to voice your weaknesses and your troubles in front of God. For He takes no pleasure in the strength of humans but delights in those who put all their hope and trust in His love.

So go to God, the One who loves you more than you could ever know. Tell Him all your troubles, hurts, wounds, and challenges. Allow Him to love you, to give you peace, and to comfort you with His words.

I come to You, Lord, seeking Your face, love, peace, and understanding.

PRAYER JAR INSPIRATION:

God's immense love for me never wavers.

GOD SO LOVED

For God so loved the world that he gave his one and only Son,
that whoever believes in him shall not perish but have eternal life.

JOHN 3:16 NIV

Chances are you know this verse by heart. Yet when is the last time you really allowed the power of its words to penetrate your mind, body, soul, and spirit?

Let's do so now. Let's take it apart and see what it may be telling us right now.

"God." The Master of all creation. The supernatural Being with the ultimate plan. "So loved the world." God so loved *you*. *You* who are part of this world and the next. So great was His love for you that "he gave." He didn't hold back—never holds back—whatever you need. So He gave. "His one and only Son." Imagine having only one of something. So precious, so loved. Yet still, God gave this Son, *His* Son, His one and only Son. "That whoever." Any person. Anyone. *You.* "Believes." Hopes in, accepts, trusts. "In him." Not in just anyone but in Him. "Shall not perish but have eternal life." Shall never die. Ever.

God so loved *you* that He gave His only Son so *you* who believe should live forever. Take these words to heart today and in all your tomorrows.

Lord, I put all of myself, all my hope in Your forever love!

PRAYER JAR INSPIRATION:

God's love for me is eternal.

30

DEVELOPING HOPE

*Hope [in God's promises] never disappoints us, because
God's love has been abundantly poured out within our
hearts through the Holy Spirit who was given to us.*

ROMANS 5:5 AMP

The Bible tells us that we're to rejoice when we have problems. Why? Because those problems "help us develop endurance. And endurance develops strength of character, and character strengthens our confident hope of salvation" (Romans 5:3–4 NLT).

Let's face it. This is a fallen world. And we will continue to have our share of problems here on earth. Yet still, even in those trials, we're never to forget that God does love us and that we still have His grace on us. Those things remain true. It's just that God allows troubles because He wants us to become more and more like His Son. And just as He did with Jesus, God will use our trials for our good—*if* we trust Him to do so, *if* we continue to hope in His promises.

So today, even in your trials, remember God's great love for you. Know that whatever is happening will come to some good. All you need to do is trust. To hope.

*God, I hope not in man nor beast nor money
nor success but in You and Your great love!*

PRAYER JAR INSPIRATION:

*I can rejoice in all days, in all ways, for God
loves me. And I hope in His promises!*

31

A CONDUIT OF LOVE

If I speak with the tongues of men and of angels, but have not love
[for others growing out of God's love for me], then I have become only
a noisy gong or a clanging cymbal [just an annoying distraction].

1 CORINTHIANS 13:1 AMP

Do you really believe God loves you? Do you believe in that love
with all your heart, spirit, soul, and mind? Because if you don't believe
in that superabundant love God has for you, you're going to have a
difficult time loving others.

Perhaps you feel as if love is a hopeless idea. Perhaps you were
deprived of love or lost a loved one in the early years of your life.
Perhaps you loved another and your love wasn't returned. The pain
of that experience has put you off of love.

If any of these possibilities rings true, remember who you are:
God's creation. The person He wants to have an intimate relationship
with. The person He loved even before you became aware of Him.

Hope and have faith in God's love. Then, knowing love is forever
flowing out to you, become a conduit of that love, pouring it out to
everyone you meet. Soon you will be overflowing with love.

Lord, give me love for others.

PRAYER JAR INSPIRATION:

I am a conduit of God's great love.

ALL THINGS

*Love bears all things [regardless of what comes], believes all things
[looking for the best in each one], hopes all things [remaining steadfast
during difficult times], endures all things [without weakening].*

1 Corinthians 13:7 AMP

This verse seems like a tall order. It's difficult to love someone, to look for the best in every person, no matter what that person does. It can be hard to hope, especially when people are behaving as if they've never even heard of love—for God, themselves, or others! It seems arduous to endure every difficulty no matter how hard, to stay strong in love no matter what happens.

Yet if you really think about it, doing these things—bearing all, believing there is good in everyone, hoping for the best, and enduring whatever comes your way—is actually a wonderful plan! It's a great way to escape the grief and negativity the opposite attitude would hold.

So start today! Allow the love that God has poured into you to help you bear, believe, hope, and endure. Then take note of how your loving attitude and outlook changes your life—for the better, for the best, for God.

Lord, help my love to bear, believe, hope, and endure all things!

PRAYER JAR INSPIRATION:

*With God's love in me and pouring out of me,
I can bear, believe, hope, and endure anything!*

THE GREATEST

*And now there remain: faith [abiding trust in God and His
promises], hope [confident expectation of eternal salvation],
love [unselfish love for others growing out of God's love for me],
these three [the choicest graces]; but the greatest of these is love.*

1 CORINTHIANS 13:13 AMP

There are three things essential to a Christian. The first is faith. Only
by believing in Jesus Christ can you get near to God, have your sins
forgiven and forgotten, and find eternal life.

Then you need hope. Only by expecting that God will come
through on all His promises to you will you keep going and get to
the eventual finish line.

And lastly is love. Love is greater than both faith and hope. For
there will come a day when your faith will actually become sight,
and when all that you hoped for is finally realized because all God's
promises have become a reality. Yet love will continue into eternity.
Love is God, and God will abide forever.

Today and every day, look to your faith for guidance and security.
Persevere in the hope of God's promises. But most of all, live in and
give love—to God, yourself, and others—knowing that love is the
greatest thing in heaven and on earth.

Today, Lord, I choose to live in faith, hope, and love.

PRAYER JAR INSPIRATION:

Nothing is greater than love.

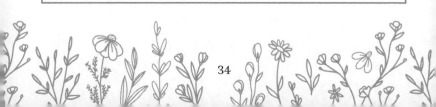

BEING LOVE

*Love the Lord your God with all your heart, with all your soul, with all
your strength, and with all your mind; and your neighbor as yourself.*

LUKE 10:27 HCSB

A scholar asked Jesus what he needed to do to have eternal life. Jesus
told him he must love God with all his heart, soul, strength, and
mind and love his neighbor as he loved himself. In fact, all the laws
of Moses, including the Ten Commandments, could be summed up
in that one sentence!

Yet the scholar still needed clarity. He wanted to know who his
neighbor was. So Jesus told him the parable of the Good Samaritan
(Luke 10:30–37). In this story, Jesus makes it clear that if you see
someone in need, passing by that person is not an option. You must be
like the Good Samaritan and help those who need it. That may mean
not getting done what you wanted to get done that day. That may mean
allowing yourself to be distracted and your schedule to be interrupted.

This life isn't all about you and your plans. It's about being there
for those in need, knowing God will enable you and equip you to help
others. Love your neighbor by caring, stopping, and responding. Today.

Lord, who would You have me help today?

PRAYER JAR INSPIRATION:

Hope for all resides in neighborly love.

DARING TO HOPE

*Yet I still dare to hope when I remember this: The faithful love of the L*ORD *never ends! His mercies never cease. Great is his faithfulness; his mercies begin afresh each morning.*

SMALL_CAPS

LAMENTATIONS 3:21–23 NLT

It's not easy being a godly human. So many times and in so many areas of our lives, we find ourselves tripping up, doing or saying the wrong thing. Or, in our struggle to support ourselves and our loved ones, we may find ourselves putting our work, our need to earn money, or our desire to attain the good life above our faith, families, and friends. Soon we realize how little we've done for God, how often we've ignored our families, and how many of our friendships have fallen by the wayside.

Yet we can hang on to the hope that God's love is never ending. His loving-kindness never wanes. His faithfulness to us is immense, immeasurable, infinite. His mercies are new every morning. Every day we have a fresh start.

Make that day today. Take hold of this morning's freely given do-over from God. Love God, yourself, and others like you've never done before. Ask Him to open your mind and heart to whoever needs encouragement, love, forgiveness, or mercy. Spread the hope that everyone can have a fresh start.

Thank You, Lord, for Your abundant love, mercy, and faithfulness!

PRAYER JAR INSPIRATION:

Today I will make a new start at _____.

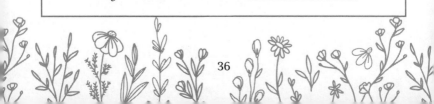

36

FLOODED WITH LOVE

Your left arm would be under my head, and your right arm would embrace me. . . . Love is as strong as death, its jealousy as enduring as the grave. Love flashes like fire, the brightest kind of flame. Many waters cannot quench love, nor can rivers drown it.

SONG OF SOLOMON 8:3, 6–7 NLT

There may be days when you doubt you are loved by anyone in heaven or on earth. Or perhaps you have grown so distant from God that you're ashamed to come back. Having fallen out of the fold, you're not sure how to get back in. Maybe you think or feel that God's love has flown not just from you but from the entire world. If so, think and feel again.

God, who is love personified, loves you like no one else can. He is not some distant God you cannot reach. He is with you, beside you, holding you in His arms!

And that love He feels for you is as strong as death. No amount of water can extinguish the flame of love God lavishes on you. No floods can drown it.

Today, hope in the strength and durability of God's abundant love. Allow it to pour into your heart and mind. Be flooded with love.

In the bounty of Your love, Lord, I hope and live.

PRAYER JAR INSPIRATION:

I'm flooded with God's unending love.

SUPPORTED BY LOVE

Unless the LORD had helped me, I would soon have settled in the silence of the grave. I cried out, "I am slipping!" but your unfailing love, O LORD, supported me. When doubts filled my mind, your comfort gave me renewed hope and cheer.

PSALM 94:17–19 NLT

In this material world, it's easy to get lost in the minutiae of life—to find yourself not living your dream but dreaming your life. And then something happens. As you come up against real and unexpected trouble, your heart skips a beat. You suddenly find yourself crying out to God, "Lord, I'm slipping! Catch me! Hold me up! Help me stand!"

And in that moment, God will respond. He will reach out with that unfailing love of His in which you've set much of your hope. That love will lift you up, keep you from going down into the abyss.

When you begin to doubt not just God's love but His very existence, cry out to Him again. When you do, He will comfort you, hold you, sit with you until your hope and cheer are restored.

Hope in the Lord's help. And you will find not just your footing but all the comfort and love you could ask for.

Hold me up, Lord, with Your unceasing and unfailing love!

PRAYER JAR INSPIRATION:

God is always there to support me with His love, to renew my hope!

NO-FAULT LOVE

Always be humble and gentle. Be patient with each other,
making allowance for each other's faults because of your love.

EPHESIANS 4:2 NLT

It's easy to brag about your abilities and to be hard on others. . .to want to get in the last word or to lose your patience. . .to continually berate others because of their faults and to lift yourself up in your own eyes. But God would have you do the exact opposite.

You belong to a God who Himself is the personification of love. And as such, He wants you to be humble, to put others before yourself. To be gentle, not abrasive or harsh. To be patient with others. To love them despite their faults—just as God loves you despite yours. Not sometimes but *all the time*. Hello!

This kind of loving is going to take energy. You're going to have to dig deep to keep calm, cool, and collected when others provoke you. But with God in your heart and the knowledge that you too are not perfect, you can do what you are called to do. And all because you belong to the Master of love who calls you to love others—no matter what.

God, help me cling to the hope that You and Your love
can make me a humble, gentle, and patient woman.

PRAYER JAR INSPIRATION:

Lord, overwhelm me with love for others.

THE NEW YOU

Put on the new [spiritual] self who is being continually renewed in
true knowledge in the image of Him who created the new self. . . .
Put on a heart of compassion, kindness, humility, gentleness, and
patience. . . . Beyond all these things put on and wrap yourselves in
[unselfish] love, which is the perfect bond of unity [for everything is
bound together in agreement when each one seeks the best for others].

COLOSSIANS 3:10, 12, 14 AMP

What would your world be like if you dressed in a new spiritual outfit, one like Jesus wore? What would change if each morning you adorned yourself with compassion, kindness, humility, gentleness, patience, and above all, unselfish love? How would these changes change not only you but the people around you—family, friends, and strangers?

When you became a follower of Christ, you gained an entirely new wardrobe, one that will never go out of style and you will never outgrow. Each morning, take stock of what you have clothed yourself with. Then step into your world looking like Jesus. And notice the hope you exude.

Help me, Lord, to be as You are, to see as You see,
to hope as You hope, to do as You do. In Your name.

PRAYER JAR INSPIRATION:

Lord, wrap me in Your selfless loving-kindness.

LOVE AS GOD LOVES

"Do to others as you would like them to do to you. If you love only those who love you, why should you get credit for that? Even sinners love those who love them! And if you do good only to those who do good to you, why should you get credit? Even sinners do that much!"

LUKE 6:31–33 NLT

Sometimes we feel pretty good about ourselves and our relationships with others. We pat ourselves on the back for helping a nice woman with her groceries, sharing our garden produce with our kind neighbors, or shoveling snow from the sidewalk of a fellow churchgoer. It's easy to be nice to nice people. It's much harder to be nice to nasty people. Yet we are called to love *all* humans—even those who do not share our beliefs, values, or customs. . .even if they don't love us back!

So what's a woman to do? Well, the next time someone cuts you off in traffic, ask God to bless her instead of blaring your horn. Consider baking some cookies for the neighbor who is more contentious than conscientious. Or find a way to anonymously help out the unbeliever who just lost her job because she stole from the petty cash.

Lord, help me lovingly do to others as I would have them do to me.

PRAYER JAR INSPIRATION:

My hope and reward lie in loving as God loves.

STIRRING UP LOVE
AND BLESSINGS

*The mouth of the righteous is a fountain of life and his words of
wisdom are a source of blessing, but the mouth of the wicked conceals
violence and evil. Hatred stirs up strife, but love covers and overwhelms
all transgressions [forgiving and overlooking another's faults].*

<small>PROVERBS 10:11–12 AMP</small>

Words carry great power. The words that come out of our mouths
can either bless or curse, build up or cut down, stir up love within
hearts or suffocate others with hatred. Where do your words fall on
this spectrum?

Today, keep watch over the things you say. Consider the effect they
have on others. Ask God to help you stop before you speak. To pause
and, if needed, turn what would have been a curse into a blessing.
Speak words of love and encouragement. Doing so will change not
only the lives of others but your own as well.

*Help me pause before I prattle, Lord. To speak words alive with life.
To send out blessings and curtail curses. To love well, and in doing so,
to forgive and overlook the faults of others. In Jesus' name, amen.*

PRAYER JAR INSPIRATION:

Lord of all, make my mouth a fountain of wisdom, blessing, and love.

CONSTANT LOVE

*I will give You thanks with all my heart; I will sing Your praise before
the heavenly beings. I will bow down toward Your holy temple
and give thanks to Your name for Your constant love and truth.*

P<small>SALM</small> 138:1–2 <small>HCSB</small>

Make today a day that you thank God from the heart for His constant
love and truth. Why? Because love is the greatest thing we have going.
Love covers a multitude of sins, gives us joy, helps us heal, and blesses
us beyond belief. For. . .God. . .is. . .love (1 John 4:16).

God loved us so much that He allowed His Son, His one and
only Son, to die for us "while we were still sinners" (Romans 5:8
HCSB)! That means that when we were still selfish, mean, and nasty
miscreants, God sent His precious Son to be whipped, stripped,
beaten, mocked, and nailed to a cross. *That* is love. A very precious,
all-giving, and forgiving love.

So give your love back to God in the form of praise and thanks-
giving. Thank Him that He keeps loving you, no matter how often
you misstep or misspeak. In doing so, you will be reminding yourself
of how wondrous, gracious, and mercy-filled God's love is.

I thank You, Lord, for Your constant love. In Jesus' name, amen.

PRAYER JAR INSPIRATION:

God's love for me will never die!

RETURN TO SENDER

"There was a man who had two sons. And the younger of them said to his father, 'Father, give me the share of property that is coming to me.' And he divided his property between them."

LUKE 15:11–12 ESV

God has given His children everything. And He has done so quite willingly.

Yet many do not know or recognize that fact. They just see the blessings that God provides—food, air, land, water, shelter, love, and so forth—as something they deserve. Something that is owed to them.

Such people may live high off the hog, squandering all God's blessings. And then when tough times come, when they are in need, they see themselves as their only resource. They hire themselves out for a job that gives them neither joy nor ample provision. They begin to long to eat what a pig is given for slop.

Hopefully, such prodigals will eventually come to their senses. They will go back home to the Provider of blessings. They will seek out the God who continually gives and continually loves.

Today, take stock of the inheritance of love you have been blessed with. Return to the holy Provider of love. Then find the pathway to bless others with that love.

Lord, thank You for blessing me with a treasure trove of love.

PRAYER JAR INSPIRATION:

*Father God, teach me how to take,
return, and spread Your precious love.*

WORTHY LOVE

"When he came to his senses, he said, 'How many of my father's hired hands have more than enough food, and here I am dying of hunger! I'll get up, go to my father, and say to him, Father, I have sinned against heaven and in your sight. I'm no longer worthy to be called your son.'"

LUKE 15:17–19 HCSB

The son who had squandered the inheritance from his father found himself in dire straits. Realizing what he had done, he decided to go back home and humbly apologize to his dad.

"But while the son was still a long way off, his father saw him and was filled with compassion. He ran, threw his arms around his neck, and kissed him" (Luke 15:20 HCSB). Before the son could even get his entire apology out, his father called for his servants to put the best robe on the boy, to slip a ring on his finger, and to shod his feet with sandals.

Just as the prodigal's father had compassion on, loved, and forgave his son, your Father God has compassion on, loves, and forgives you. If you've strayed, remember that God's love for you never dies.

Thank You, Father God, for loving me,
no matter how unworthy I feel myself to be.

PRAYER JAR INSPIRATION:

Lord, help me not squander my inheritance of love.

LOST, THEN FOUND

"Son, you are always with me, and all that is mine is yours.
It was fitting to celebrate and be glad, for this your brother
was dead, and is alive; he was lost, and is found."

LUKE 15:31–32 ESV

When the prodigal son returned, his father rejoiced over his return. He ordered his servants to dress him in a robe and to put a ring on his finger and sandals on his feet. Then he ordered a grand feast to be cooked and served to celebrate that his son who was once lost was now found.

But the dutiful older brother became miffed and refused to share in his younger brother's welcome-home dinner. So the father went out to plead with him. The older told his dad how good he had been, how well he had served his father and obeyed him. Yet he never got such a feast.

Some of us have been dutiful to God from the beginning. Others have not. Yet we all share in the joy the Father displays to the lost who are found and the found who stick around, praising the One whose love and hope for us never ceases.

Father God, help me not to begrudge or judge
Your love and joy for the lost who become found.

PRAYER JAR INSPIRATION:

Make me a woman who rejoices when a lost
follower rediscovers Your love and protection!

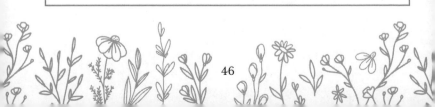

HOPE
for Forgiveness

Whether it's forgiving someone else or forgiving ourselves, most people hope for forgiveness. But we don't have to hope for forgiveness. It's offered to us freely because of Christ's death on the cross.

With forgiveness come healing and a release of guilt. If we have hurt someone and have asked for their forgiveness, we hope they will forgive us. Even if they don't, though, we know that we have done the right thing.

If someone hurts us and doesn't seek our forgiveness, we are instructed in the Bible to forgive anyway, which will give us a sense of release. "If ye forgive men their trespasses, your heavenly Father will also forgive you" (Matthew 6:14 KJV).

Forgiveness isn't about overlooking the problem or evading an issue. It doesn't mean approval of what someone else did that was sinful or caused us pain. It doesn't mean all the consequences of sin are canceled. Forgiveness begins in the heart and eventually works its way outward. Forgiving someone else or asking God to forgive us for things we've done wrong allows us to move on and grow in our walk with Him. If we are going to follow Jesus, then we must forgive others as God has forgiven us. "And be ye kind one to another, tenderhearted, forgiving one another, even as God for Christ's sake hath forgiven you" (Ephesians 4:32 KJV).

MUCH FORGIVEN, MUCH LOVE

A woman in the town who was a sinner found out
that Jesus was reclining at the table in the Pharisee's
house. She brought an alabaster jar of fragrant oil.

LUKE 7:37 HCSB

Simon, a Pharisee, invited Jesus to eat at his home. While Jesus sat down at the table, a woman known to be a sinner entered. Saying nothing, she wept and began washing His feet with her tears. Next, she used her hair to wipe His feet, kissed them, and anointed them.

Simon the Pharisee remarked that if Jesus were a prophet, He would know the woman touching Him was a sinner.

Hearing Simon's comment, Jesus addressed him directly, saying, "Simon, I have something to tell you." Simon said, "Oh? Tell me" (Luke 7:40 MSG).

Jesus then told Simon about a moneylender who had two clients. One owed him five hundred pieces of silver; the other fifty. Neither could repay him, so he forgave them and canceled both debts. Jesus asked Simon: "Which of the two would be more grateful?" (Luke 7:42 MSG).

Simon answered, "I suppose the one who owed him the most money."

Today, think about how much your Lord has forgiven you. Then tell Him how much you love Him for that.

Lord, open my eyes and mind so that I may
see and understand how much I owe You!

PRAYER JAR INSPIRATION:

God has so graciously forgiven me.

THE PEACE OF FORGIVENESS

"I tell you, her sins—and they are many—have been forgiven, so she has shown me much love. But a person who is forgiven little shows only little love." Then Jesus said to the woman, "Your sins are forgiven." . . . "Your faith has saved you; go in peace."

LUKE 7:47–48, 50 NLT

The Pharisee named Simon had never offered to wash the dust from Jesus' feet when He entered his home. But this sinful woman had washed them with her tears and wiped them with her hair.

Simon had not greeted Jesus with a kiss, yet this sinful woman had not stopped kissing His feet. Simon had not anointed Jesus' head with oil, yet this sinful woman had anointed His feet with expensive perfume.

Because this woman's many sins were forgiven, she demonstrated much love to the One who had forgiven her. In response, Jesus turned to the woman and said not only "your sins are forgiven" but "your faith has saved you; go in peace" (Luke 7:48, 50 NLT).

Jesus' observation turned the world upside down. The believing yet sinful woman was more gracious and loving to Him than the man of religion.

Be as this woman. Put your hope and faith in the fact that God has forgiven you. Then go in peace.

My hope and faith lie in You, Jesus, the forgiver of my sins.

PRAYER JAR INSPIRATION:

I can have peace because Jesus forgives me.

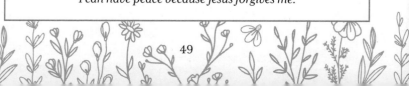

A BIG ASK

*"I say to you who listen: Love your enemies, do what is good to
those who hate you, bless those who curse you, pray for those
who mistreat you. . . . Forgive, and you will be forgiven."*

LUKE 6:27–28, 37 HCSB

Jesus speaks to anyone who will listen, explaining the love He wants
us to show each other as well as the forgiveness He wants to extend.
For humankind, these things appear to be a big ask.

Yet Jesus urges us to bless the person who curses us. To the one
who strikes us on one cheek, we're to offer the other. To the one who
takes our coat, we're to offer our shirt. To the one who begs from us,
we're to give what we have. To the one who takes a possession from
us, we're not to demand its return. To the one who needs forgiveness,
we're to forgive—then we too will be forgiven.

Although these ideas may on the surface seem difficult, in practice
the result is delightful. Taking the high road leaves us with far more
hope and joy than we find wallowing in the mud of the low road.

*Show me who I can love and forgive today,
Lord, while asking nothing in return!*

PRAYER JAR INSPIRATION:

*My hope for myself and humankind is found in
loving the unlovable, forgiving the unforgivable.*

SEVEN TIMES SEVENTY

*"Lord, how many times could my brother sin against
me and I forgive him? As many as seven times?"*

MATTHEW 18:21 HCSB

Your friend has done it again. You told her something in confidence,
and now you've found out she's shared that secret with another! This
is the seventh time she's done this! You sigh heavily, roll your eyes,
and say to God, "Really, Lord? I have to forgive her *again*? When is
enough enough?"

Apparently, never.

The disciple Peter wanted an exact number of times he had to forgive
another person. And he thought he was being generous doing so seven
times, especially considering that three times was the accepted norm in
Judaism (Job 33:29–30; Amos 1:3, 2:6). But Jesus shocked him (and us)
by saying he should forgive seventy times seven, which comes to 490
times. Yet, if you're truly a disciple of Jesus, you won't be keeping count.

Once again, Jesus seems to be asking us to do the impossible. Yet
it is because of Him that we *can* do the impossible! So what are you
to do in the example we began with? Forgive the secret sharer again.
But maybe from now on, forgo telling her something you don't want
anyone else to know.

*Lord, give me the power, patience, and passion to
continually forgive others as You continually forgive me!*

PRAYER JAR INSPIRATION:

God will give me the strength to forgive and forgive and forgive.

UNCONDITIONAL FORGIVENESS

"Forgive your brother from your heart."
MATTHEW 18:35 ESV

Because we are forgiven by God, we must forgive each other. Jesus makes this crystal clear in the parable of the unforgiving servant.

There once was a king who wanted to settle accounts with those who'd borrowed money from him. One of his debtors owed him millions of dollars. But he couldn't pay. So the king commanded that the debtor—as well as his wife, children, and possessions—be sold to make good on what was owed. The debtor prostrated himself before the king, begging him to be patient until he paid back all monies owed. Filled with sympathy for the man, the king forgave him and ordered his release.

This same man then went to another man who owed him a few thousand dollars and demanded payment. This second man begged for the other's patience. But he was refused, arrested, and put in jail until the debt could be paid in full. When the king found out what had happened, he sent the initial debtor to prison until all could be repaid.

Jesus said, "So also my heavenly Father will do to every one of you, if you do not forgive your brother from your heart" (Matthew 18:35 ESV).

To whom do you need to extend loving forgiveness?

Lord, make me a woman who not only
forgives but does so with all her heart.

PRAYER JAR INSPIRATION:

May I forgive not just in words but in love.

SHADOW OF UNFORGIVENESS

"Whenever you stand praying, if you have anything against anyone, forgive him [drop the issue, let it go], so that your Father who is in heaven will also forgive you your transgressions and wrongdoings [against Him and others]."

MARK 11:25 AMP

Have you ever gone to God in prayer but found yourself stumbling for the right words? Or perhaps you didn't exactly feel like praying, so you just lifted up an SOS prayer (a short and sweet plea for help) and went on your way?

If you're struggling to find the words to pray to God or you just don't feel you're in the mood to speak with Him, chances are there's a barrier between thee and He. And that barrier could be the fact that there's someone in your life you have not forgiven.

That's why Jesus makes it clear that if you're praying and there is a shadow of unforgiveness blocking His light, you need to forgive that person. For only then can your Father God forgive you.

Today, before you pray, take stock of what is in your heart. If there is any shade obscuring God's light, consider who you may need to forgive. Then do so. And you too will receive full forgiveness.

Help me, Lord, to forgive others so that You may forgive me.

PRAYER JAR INSPIRATION:

I hope and pray God's light would lead me to full forgiveness.

JESUS' PRAYER
OF FORGIVENESS

*When they came to a place called The Skull, they nailed him to the cross.
And the criminals were also crucified—one on his right and one on his
left. Jesus said, "Father, forgive them, for they don't know what they
are doing." And the soldiers gambled for his clothes by throwing dice.*

<small>LUKE 23:33–34 NLT</small>

Imagine being one of Jesus' female followers, those who could only pray
and watch from a distance as Jesus was deserted and denied by His
own disciples, then arrested, tried, spit on, struck, scourged, stripped,
mocked, and crucified by those who knew no better.

And in the middle of all this human heartlessness comes Jesus'
amazing prayer to His Father: "Father, forgive them, for they don't
know what they are doing."

Jesus never gave us any challenge that He Himself did not face.
If He can forgive everything that was done against Him, surely we
can forgive everything that is done against us.

Today, as you reflect on those who have injured you, look at what you
endured in the light of what Jesus suffered. Then ask Him for the strength
to forgive others, regardless of whether they knew what they were doing.

*In Your name, Lord, I pray for the strength to
forgive everything that has been done against me.*

PRAYER JAR INSPIRATION:

*Jesus, You are the Lord of the impossible.
Help me forgive the seemingly unforgivable.*

NOBODY'S PERFECT

We are made right with God by placing our faith in Jesus Christ.
And this is true for everyone who believes, no matter who we are.
For everyone has sinned; we all fall short of God's glorious standard.

ROMANS 3:22–23 NLT

It's true. You are not perfect. No one is. That's why we needed Jesus to willingly sacrifice His life and, in doing so, to free us from the penalty of sin (Romans 3:25).

Before Jesus came, people did their best to follow the laws God made. But they fell short. Continually. Very short. Consider David, the apple of God's eye. Even as close as he was to God, he slept with a married woman. Then, when he learned she was pregnant, he set things up so that her husband would be killed in battle and he could claim her for his own!

When we look at ourselves, at how much we fall short in God's eyes, it makes it easier to forgive those who have fallen short in our eyes. Today, humbly forgive those who have disappointed or wronged you in some way, reminding yourself that no one but Jesus is perfect.

I ask for Your forgiveness, Lord, as I forgive others,
knowing we all fall short in Your eyes.

PRAYER JAR INSPIRATION:

My own imperfections urge me to forgive those in others.

PLEASING THE SPIRIT

Do not bring sorrow to God's Holy Spirit by the way you live. Remember, he has identified you as his own, guaranteeing that you will be saved on the day of redemption. . . . Instead, be kind to each other, tenderhearted, forgiving one another, just as God through Christ has forgiven you.

EPHESIANS 4:30, 32 NLT

When you become a follower of Christ, you are to change some of your ways and embark on a new life. If you've had some trouble in that regard, do not despair! There is hope!

Every day, Jesus gives you the opportunity to "throw off your old sinful nature and your former way of life" (Ephesians 4:22 NLT) and to "put on your new nature, created to be like God" (Ephesians 4:24 NLT).

That means you need to stop telling lies and letting anger control you. Your words are to be words of encouragement, not abuse. And even more than that, you're not to grieve the Spirit. Instead, you're to be a woman of compassion and forgiveness.

Today, make God and His Spirit happy. Be nice, gentle, compassionate, and forgiving to others, just as God is to you.

Lord, make me a woman pleasing to You, Your Spirit, and others, being kind, gentle, compassionate, and forgiving.

PRAYER JAR INSPIRATION:

My hope lies in gladdening God just as He gladdens me!

ABUNDANT PARDON

Seek the Lord while He may be found; call on Him [for salvation] while He is near. Let the wicked leave (behind) his way and the unrighteous man his thoughts; and let him return to the Lord, and He will have compassion (mercy) on him, and to our God, for He will abundantly pardon.

ISAIAH 55:6–7 AMP

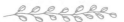

Even when we mess up, we can seek out and call on God. We can leave behind our misdeeds, step off the wrong path we've embarked on, change our thoughts, return to God—and He will take us back in. As prodigal daughters, we can still run into the open arms of our loving God and be folded into His loving and forgiving embrace.

At the same time, we need to find a way to forgive ourselves—and perhaps ask others to forgive us for how we've wronged them. In asking God for forgiveness, forgiving ourselves, and apologizing to others, we will find the freedom to look forward to better days.

In what areas of life do you need to seek God and His forgiveness? Is there any forgiveness you need to extend to yourself or ask of others? If so, ask God to help you. In His mercy, He will.

I call on You, Lord, seeking Your forgiveness.

PRAYER JAR INSPIRATION:

In seeking God, I find hope, mercy, and an abundance of forgiveness.

LETTING GO

From the depths of despair, O Lord, I call for your help. Hear my cry, O Lord. Pay attention to my prayer. Lord, if you kept a record of our sins, who, O Lord, could ever survive?

PSALM 130:1–3 NLT

Sometimes the things we have done can lead us to a state of despair. So burdened are we by our missteps that we can barely lift our heads. And we begin to wonder how many pages of our misdeeds God has on file. How many will He forgive?

Fortunately for us, we have a Lord who is "merciful and gracious, slow to anger and abounding in steadfast love" (Psalm 103:8 ESV). He's a God who doesn't "deal with us according to our sins, nor repay us according to our iniquities" (Psalm 103:10 ESV). Why? Because "as high as the heavens are above the earth, so great is his steadfast love toward those who fear him; as far as the east is from the west, so far does he remove our transgressions from us" (Psalm 103:11–12 ESV).

So, woman of God, go to your Lord and confess your misdeeds. Remember that He is the One who loves you, who longs for you to unburden your heart so that you can let go of despair and embrace all He has planned for you.

Lord, here's what happened. . . .

PRAYER JAR INSPIRATION:

God's abundant love and mercy are mine!

THAT EXTRA MILE

"If anyone forces you to go one mile, go with him two."
MATTHEW 5:41 HCSB

Jesus was wholeheartedly into forgiveness. He wanted His followers to completely forget about exacting revenge on those who had wronged them. He told them, "You have heard that it was said, An eye for an eye and a tooth for a tooth. But I tell you, don't resist an evildoer. . . . If anyone forces you to go one mile, go with him two" (Matthew 5:38–39, 41 HCSB).

Yet to go that extra mile, you may need to figure out a way to forgive the person who has wronged you. On occasion that can be very difficult. It may take you time to be able to pardon the wrongdoer's actions. That's okay. Just don't wait too long or your unforgiveness may transform itself into bitterness. And that's definitely not where you want to be.

Today, consider who it is that you have yet to forgive. Then, going forward, try to live so that your love for God and His free-flowing love and mercy to you will keep your vengefulness in check and lead to your going that extra mile.

Help me, Lord, to go that extra mile with people who wrong me.

PRAYER JAR INSPIRATION:

God, help me transform Your mercy to me into forgiveness for others, no matter how much they have wounded me.

PATIENCE AND TOLERANCE

The servant of the Lord must not participate in quarrels, but must be kind to everyone [even-tempered, preserving peace, and he must be], skilled in teaching, patient and tolerant when wronged. He must correct those who are in opposition with courtesy and gentleness in the hope that God may grant that they will repent and be led to the knowledge of the truth [accurately understanding and welcoming it].

2 TIMOTHY 2:24–25 AMP

You are not just a daughter of God but a servant of the Lord. And as such, you are to walk as He walked, talk as He talked.

So, you're not to be quarrelsome. Instead, find a way to be kind to everyone. Teach them where the truth of a particular matter lies. And overall, be patient with people, even those who are difficult and have wronged you in some way. In doing so, you will not only be keeping and promoting peace but hopefully providing some much-needed space for God to change people's hearts.

Remember how gentle and kind, loving and patient your Savior is. Then go. Do the same, praying for God's help along the way.

God, please gift me with more tolerance and patience around difficult people. Help me promote Your peace and love.

PRAYER JAR INSPIRATION:

My hope of patience and tolerance lies in God's abundant and available supply!

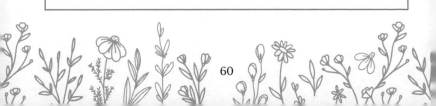

FORGIVENESS PRAYER

Do not remember the rebellious sins of my youth. Remember me in the light of your unfailing love, for you are merciful, O Lord. The Lord is good and does what is right; he shows the proper path to those who go astray. . . . O Lord, forgive my many, many sins.

PSALM 25:7–8, 11 NLT

We know that God is good and that His mercy and love are never ending. Yet it can be difficult to tell Him all the missteps we have made, because when we confess, we must admit them to ourselves.

Fortunately, we have the book of Psalms to help us. These verses from Psalm 25 are a prime example of how we can use what others have written to help us approach God in prayer.

The psalmist, David, asked God to see beyond his sins, to be viewed by God in the light of His love. He reminded God and himself that He is good and right and would show David how to get back on track. Most of all, he asked God to forgive his many sins.

Today, ask the Spirit to help you use the Psalms to address God in prayer as you seek His forgiveness. Take note of what happens when you do.

Lord, "do not remember the rebellious sins of my youth. . . ."

PRAYER JAR INSPIRATION:

Help me, Lord, to find the psalm prayer that fits me.

61

C - O - N - F - E - S - S - I - O - N
SPELLS RELIEF

Finally, I confessed all my sins to you and stopped trying to hide my guilt. I said to myself, "I will confess my rebellion to the LORD." And you forgave me! All my guilt is gone. . . . People who conceal their sins will not prosper, but if they confess and turn from them, they will receive mercy.

PSALM 32:5, PROVERBS 28:13 NLT

There is something about confession that lightens the spirit.

After an intense debate with her child, a godly mother felt awful. Some things that had come out of her mouth were making her spirit cringe. The only remedy for the shame she felt was to seek out her son, confess that what she had said was wrong, and ask for his forgiveness. Doing so took a lot of courage. But the result was relief and forgiveness for the mother as well as the bonus of a closer connection between mother and son.

The same thing happens when you confess all to God. You'll obtain not only relief for releasing your misdeeds but forgiveness as well. And you'll find your bond to God even tighter.

Lord, I'm done trying to hide my guilt, as if I could hide anything from You. So, I come to You to confess and receive Your mercy and forgiveness.

PRAYER JAR INSPIRATION:

Give me the courage to come clean with You, Lord!

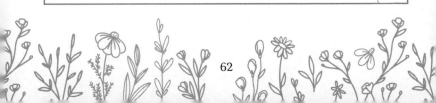

HOPE
for Happiness

As a child, I hoped things in my life would get better and I would feel happy. I didn't realize I'd been going around with a long face until one day on the school bus I was confronted by a classmate who sat next to me. I will never forget her words as she looked at me and asked, "How come you never smile?"

"There's nothing to smile about," I responded.

"Seriously?"

"If you had to live in my home, you'd understand."

"No matter how bad things are, there's always something to smile about." She pointed out the bus window. "See those flowers growing in that yard? Looking at their pretty colors makes me smile. So does listening to the birds, riding my bike, and playing games." She gave me a dimpled smile. "Stop thinking about what makes you feel sad, and look for things that will make you smile."

My eyes had been opened to the truth. When I focus on positive things, I don't have to hope for happiness. I can bring joy into my life by learning to be more cheerful. When I laugh or smile, I feel better physically, emotionally, and spiritually. I've put my hope in Jesus, for knowing Him has brought me a sense of peace and happiness.

There's a passage in the Bible that has become one of my favorite verses: "A merry heart doeth good like a medicine: but a broken spirit drieth the bones" (Proverbs 17:22 KJV).

CLOTHED WITH JOY

You have turned my mourning into joyful dancing. You have taken away my clothes of mourning and clothed me with joy, that I might sing praises to you and not be silent. O Lord my God, I will give you thanks forever!

PSALM 30:11–12 NLT

In this life, there will be some rough spots, some trials we have to endure. But those trials are what draw us ever closer to God and help us become more like His Son.

The way to endure those trials is by focusing on the fact that God is with us through them. We may have to face some enemies, but God will not let them triumph over us. We may get sick, but when we call out to God, He will restore us. We may keep falling into a pit of despair, but God will lift us out. We may have eyes full of tears tonight, but God will bring us joy, just as He brings the morning.

No matter how far down you might go, remember that God will bring you back up. Just trust in Him. Pray for help. And you will find yourself clothed with joy and giving God thanks for His deliverance.

Deliver me from this pit of despair, Lord, and lift me into Your joy!

PRAYER JAR INSPIRATION:

Even in despair, I have hope in the joy of God's deliverance.

CULTIVATING HOLY JOY

*"Go [your way], eat the rich festival food, drink the sweet drink,
and send portions to him for whom nothing is prepared; for
this day is holy to our Lord. And do not be worried, for the
joy of the LORD is your strength and your stronghold."*

NEHEMIAH 8:10 AMP

The exiled Israelites were back in Jerusalem. The walls that had been destroyed had been rebuilt. And the priests read the law of Moses to the people, helping the listeners understand God's Word. Hearing God's Word, the people realized their sins and so began to weep.

About this scene, F. B. Meyer wrote, "Contriteness of heart is wholesome and helpful, but excessive grief incapacitates us for our duties. It is well therefore to cultivate holy joy; the joy of sin forgiven, of acceptance with God, of hope that anchors us to the unseen, and that cannot be ashamed."* Therein lies our strength and stronghold.

Today, ask God to speak to your heart, to help you accept that He has forgiven you, and to help you cultivate holy joy. Then cling to that hope that anchors you to an unseen but very real God.

*Lord of love and forgiveness, of hope and compassion,
may the joy I find in You be my strength and stronghold.*

PRAYER JAR INSPIRATION:

My hope of joy lies in the unseen Lord of life.

---

* https://www.studylight.org/commentaries/eng/fbm/nehemiah-8.html

BELIEVE

*"Do not let your heart be troubled (afraid, cowardly). Believe
[confidently] in God and trust in Him, [have faith, hold on
to it, rely on it, keep going and] believe also in Me."*

JOHN 14:1 AMP

Jesus urges us not to let our hearts be troubled. Instead, we're to believe
in God and Jesus, to trust them with our loves and our lives, to hold
tightly to our faith.

Yet this world continues its attempts to toss our hearts around
and agitate our spirits. Outside forces vie for our attention, wanting
us to put our hope and trust in the world's remedies, its cures for our
seeming ills.

Fortunately, we have Jesus: the Word who never changes. The
Lord of love and compassion who refuses to let us go, who urges us
to turn to Him instead of getting swamped by worry, fear, frustration,
and terror.

Believing in the goodness and compassion of Jesus and our Father God—remembering that they have given us the Spirit to help
us cope—is all we need to find the happiness our hearts, souls, and
spirits long for. Trust in them. And you will find the joy that will
always be your strength.

It's You alone I hold on to, Lord. You are the secret of my happiness.

PRAYER JAR INSPIRATION:

*Lord, "I do believe, but help me overcome
my unbelief!" (Mark 9:24 NLT).*

OVERFLOWING JOY

"I have loved you even as the Father has loved me. Remain
in my love. When you obey my commandments, you remain
in my love, just as I obey my Father's commandments and
remain in his love. I have told you these things so that you
will be filled with my joy. Yes, your joy will overflow!"

JOHN 15:9–11 NLT

Jesus presents a somewhat easy formula for finding joy in this life:
simply obey His commandments and remain in His love. And what
are Jesus' commandments? To "love and unselfishly seek the best for
one another, just as I have loved you" (John 15:12 AMP).

Take a moment to think about it. Imagine what this world would
be like if everyone loved each other. If each man, woman, and child
unselfishly sought the best for others. The joy wouldn't just be overflowing. It would be surging!

Yet you may be asking yourself, *I am just one person. How can I even*
begin to make this a remote possibility? Begin with you. Love others—the
people around you, here and now. Begin with your world. Begin today.

Help me, Lord, to begin where I can on the road to a life
overflowing with joy by loving all those whose lives touch my own.

PRAYER JAR INSPIRATION:

My hope of joy, Lord, rests in remaining in Your love.

COMPLETE JOY

*"Until now you have not asked [the Father] for anything
in My name; but now ask and keep on asking and you
will receive, so that your joy may be full and complete."*

JOHN 16:24 AMP

Jesus told His disciples and by extension us that our joy can be full, complete, if we ask for things in His name. But what does it mean to pray in Jesus' name?

Praying in Jesus' name doesn't mean asking God for whatever you want and then just tacking on to the end of it "in Jesus' name I pray, amen." What it means is to pray to God in a way that is consistent with Jesus' character and His will.

Once again we are reminded to live our lives following in Jesus' footsteps—doing things, desiring things, asking and seeking things that He would have done, desired, asked, and sought. You can do that by thinking before you pray. Consider how Jesus would be speaking to His Father if *He* were in your shoes. Doing so will be your first step on the journey to complete joy.

*Father, this is Your daughter here. Please, teach me
how to pray to You like my Friend and Brother Jesus did.
Lead me to complete joy. In Jesus' name I pray, amen.*

PRAYER JAR INSPIRATION:

My hope is in finding joy as I live and pray Jesus' way.

SOUL TALK

Why are you in despair, O my soul? And why have you become restless and disturbed within me? Hope in God and wait expectantly for Him, for I shall again praise Him for the help of His presence.

PSALM 42:5 AMP

Some people have said that they have the most intelligent conversations when they are talking to themselves. And, as it turns out, they might be right. Studies have shown that talking to yourself indicates a higher level of intelligence!

Here, in today's verse, we overhear the psalmist talking to himself. He asks his soul, his innermost self, why it is so hopeless, restless, and anxious. Then he reminds his soul to hope in God and to wait for Him with the expectation that God *will turn things around* in a good way. When his Lord's presence provides the help the psalmist needs, his joy within and his praise without will return!

Take a cue from this psalmist. When your soul is down, when the inner woman is wearing a frown due to fear, hopelessness, restlessness, or anxiety, have a talk with her. Remind her that she can put her hope in God. He will come through in His time. He will turn things around. And she will be praising Him with all joy!

Don't despair, dear soul. God will help us.
We will be lifting our praise of Him in joy!

PRAYER JAR INSPIRATION:

My hope in God brings my soul joy!

CHOOSE!

Though the fig tree does not blossom and there is no fruit on the vines, though the yield of the olive fails and the fields produce no food, though the flock is cut off from the fold and there are no cattle in the stalls, yet I will [choose to] rejoice in the LORD; I will [choose to] shout in exultation in the [victorious] God of my salvation!

HABAKKUK 3:17–18 AMP

It's easy to be happy when everything is going well—when your pay is good, your tasks rewarding, your love life more than satisfying, your dwelling secure, your church prospering, your kids on the right track, and your body in tip-top shape. The challenge comes when something (or everything) is going off the rails—when your pay is lousy, your assignment mundane, your mate unhappy, your house flooded, your church on the brink of closing, your kids hanging with the wrong people, and your body aching.

But God wants us to choose to rejoice in Him no matter what's happening, no matter what earthly ills have befallen us. He wants us to trust in Him, not our circumstances, and to find our joy complete in Himself. For in Him alone lie all our strength, hope, and joy.

I choose to rejoice in You, Lord. You are my all in all!

PRAYER JAR INSPIRATION:

Because I choose to trust in God and not my circumstances, I have joy!

GREAT POWER

Are any of you suffering hardships? You should pray.
Are any of you happy? You should sing praises.

JAMES 5:13 NLT

If you're wondering what to do when things are going right and you are delightfully happy, James tells you to sing your praises to God. On the other hand, when all has gone wrong and your bird of happiness seems to have flown, James advises you to pray. If you're not just unhappy but sick (or you've become sick because you are unhappy), James tells you to add to your prayer power by asking the elders of your church to pray for you and anoint you with oil in Jesus' name. (See James 5:13–16.)

If you offer a prayer in faith, you will regain your health. And if you have made any missteps, they will be forgiven. Why? Not just because your God loves you, but because "the earnest prayer of a righteous person has great power and produces wonderful results" (James 5:16 NLT).

In other words, the best cure if you need healing and hope is remembering that you're not alone. That you have great power in your human hands: prayer and praise in faith!

Thank You, Lord, for blessing me with the power of prayer and praise!

PRAYER JAR INSPIRATION:

Knowing God stands with me in prayer
and praise gives me hope for happiness!

JOY-FILLED HOPE

The hope of the righteous [those of honorable character and integrity] is joy, but the expectation of the wicked [those who oppose God and ignore His wisdom] comes to nothing.

PROVERBS 10:28 AMP

Proverbs 10:27–32 gives us the pros of those who are godly and the cons of those who are wicked. And nestled among all these comparisons—all these lessons on why it's better to be godly than wicked—is verse 28 telling us that the hopes of the godly, their desires and aspirations, result in happiness and joy; but the expectations of the wicked come to naught.

There's always a chance that the hopes of those who are following God will be fulfilled. So, the godly can be joyful while they wait, living in expectation that God will move on their behalf. The wicked have no such liberty, no such expectation that God will do anything for them; in fact, chances are God will move against them.

You are a woman of the Word, a girl walking in rhythm with your Lord. Know that as you delight yourself in God, He will align your desires with His. And He will make your hopes a reality.

Thank You, Abba, for the joy that comes from my hope in You.

PRAYER JAR INSPIRATION:

God, my hopes and dreams lie in You.

PROVING A PROVERB

The king's decree gave the Jews in every city authority to unite to defend their lives. . . . And the people of Susa celebrated the new decree. The Jews were filled with joy and gladness and were honored everywhere.

ESTHER 8:11, 15–16 NLT

A wicked man named Haman, who had wormed his way into the good graces of King Xerxes of Persia, had devised a scheme so that his enemy, Mordecai the Jew, would be killed, along with all the other Jews.

But, as if to prove Proverbs 10:28—that the hopes of the righteous would be happily realized and the hopes of the dastardly ones dashed—Haman ended up being hanged, Mordecai was given Haman's former position, and the Jewish people were not slaughtered but saved! And because the Jews were saved, they were filled with joy and gladness throughout the vast Persian kingdom!

Never doubt what God promises those who follow His Way. Stick to the right path, and have faith that *you will see happiness bursting into your life* once the storm has passed.

*I believe in You and Your Word, Lord. My joy
and hope of happiness rest in You alone!*

PRAYER JAR INSPIRATION:

In His way and time, God grants happiness and joy to those He loves, proving His Word, love, and light to me over and over again.

THE ETERNAL HELPER

Don't put your confidence in powerful people; there is no help for you there. When they breathe their last, they return to the earth, and all their plans die with them. But joyful are those who have the God of Israel as their helper, whose hope is in the Lord their God.

PSALM 146:3–5 NLT

The king of Syria was tired of the prophet Elisha giving away the location of the Syrian army to the king of Israel. So the Syrian king decided to seize Elisha, who was in Dothan. He sent a huge army with chariots and horses and surrounded the city.

When Elisha's servant went outside the next morning and saw the earthly powers formed against them, he said to Elisha, "Oh, sir, what will we do now?" Elisha told him, "Don't be afraid! . . . For there are more on our side than on theirs" (2 Kings 6:15–16 NLT).

Elisha then prayed that his servant's eyes would be opened. When God answered that prayer, the servant "saw that the hillside around Elisha was filled with horses and chariots of fire" (2 Kings 6:17 NLT).

Your joy lies in the Lord of the seen *and* the unseen. Trust and hope in Him who equips and protects you beyond what you could ever think or imagine.

Thank You, Lord, for being my hope and help!

PRAYER JAR INSPIRATION:

No one can help me like God can.

GOOD NEWS

Sarah said, "God has made me laugh; all who hear [about our good news] will laugh with me." And she said, "Who would have said to Abraham that Sarah would nurse children? For I have given birth to a son by him in his old age."

GENESIS 21:6–7 AMP

God had promised an aging Abraham a son through Sarah. Sarah, having overheard the news, laughed at the idea: "After I have become shriveled up and my lord is old, will I have delight?" (Genesis 18:12 HCSB).

Yet then God's promise and her hope came to fruition. "The LORD visited Sarah as he had said, and the LORD did to Sarah as he had promised" (Genesis 21:1 ESV). In their old age, Sarah and her husband did indeed have a child. And Sarah named him Isaac, which means "laughter."

God means what He says. You can trust and hope in His promises, for He cannot lie.

And when your expectations come to fruition, you too will laugh— and others who hear about your good news will laugh with you!

Lord of all creation, may I laugh and lift my voice in praise when Your promises and my hopes come to fruition!

PRAYER JAR INSPIRATION:

I rejoice that God follows through on His promises! And I revel in His good news!

JOY OF GOD'S PRESENCE

I know the Lord is always with me. I will not be shaken, for he is right beside me. No wonder my heart is glad, and I rejoice. My body rests in safety. . . . You will show me the way of life, granting me the joy of your presence and the pleasures of living with you forever.

PSALM 16:8–9, 11 NLT

Need a little more joy in your life? Take a tip from David. Remember that God is always with you. Imagine that. The Creator and Sustainer of the universe is always at your right hand. There is nowhere you can go that He cannot follow. There is no darkness so deep that He cannot find you, reach you, and rescue you.

God is always ready to help you. To teach you and guide you. To make sure you are on the right path, the one He designed for you from the beginning of time. He will show you how to do whatever needs to be done. If you allow Him, He will work right through you to accomplish things you never thought possible.

Open your eyes and your heart. Let God be an integral part of your life. And you will discover the joy of His presence today and every day to come.

Because You are with me, Lord, I can live in joy.

PRAYER JAR INSPIRATION:

Heart, open yourself up to God's presence, and experience the joy it brings!

REJOICE!

Let the godly rejoice. Let them be glad in God's presence. Let them be filled with joy. Sing praises to God and to his name! Sing loud praises to him who rides the clouds. His name is the LORD—rejoice in his presence! . . . Praise the Lord; praise God our savior! For each day he carries us in his arms. Our God is a God who saves! The Sovereign LORD rescues us from death.

PSALM 68:3–4, 19–20 NLT

When you are working and resting, playing and reading, sunning and funning in the presence of God, you cannot help but be filled with joy.

Today, sing out your praises to the Lord. Look up to the clouds and imagine Him riding them, soaring across the sky, making things right in the lives of His people—all while remaining at your side, working within you, empowering you, helping you.

No matter what burden you may be carrying today, brush it aside. For there is One much greater, much more powerful than you. He is the supreme Being who carries you in His arms. Every day. He will not let you go. He will save you.

Believe. Rejoice.

I can feel You carrying me in this moment, Lord. Hold me close!

PRAYER JAR INSPIRATION:

God carries me in His arms each day. Praise to God!

GOD IS AWESOME!

Father to the fatherless, defender of widows—this is God, whose dwelling is holy. God places the lonely in families; he sets the prisoners free and gives them joy. . . . God is awesome in his sanctuary. The God of Israel gives power and strength to his people. Praise be to God!

PSALM 68:5–6, 35 NLT

Someday you may lose your parents, your spouse, or your bestie. Yet even then you need not despair. There is always One who remains with you. His name is the Lord.

He was with you before you were born, planning out your life, making things ready for your role in His plan. He is the One who timed your entrance on the earthly stage. He is and will remain with you 24-7.

When you are alone, God places you in a family. When you are imprisoned, He sets you free. When you are weak, He gives you power and strength.

Why does God do all this? Because you are His beloved daughter. In this awesome God who cares for you like no other, may you not only rejoice but offer your eternal thanks!

I lift up my thanks to the God who is with me and cares for me eternally!

PRAYER JAR INSPIRATION:

Lord, I reach out today for Your gift of unending joy.

78

UNFAILING LOVE

The LORD watches over those who fear him, those who rely on his unfailing love. . . . We put our hope in the LORD. He is our help and our shield. In him our hearts rejoice, for we trust in his holy name. Let your unfailing love surround us, LORD, for our hope is in you alone.

PSALM 33:18, 20–22 NLT

We've been told not to hope in anything or anyone but God. But sometimes that can be difficult. God is unseen, and it takes faith to believe the unseen will come to our aid. We may begin to rely on finances, other people, or other powers. But soon we come to realize that the Lord is the God of abundance, more powerful than people, things, or institutions.

So today, remember that God is watching over you. That His love will never fail you. That He alone can help and protect you.

Today, rejoice in the God of gods—the all-powerful, all-loving Being who created you. The One who will always stand by you, never fail you. Put your hope in Him alone. Trust in His holy name.

Remind me in this moment, Lord, that You are loving me, helping me, shielding me. That I can trust in You. May I feel Your presence, Lord, as my heart rejoices in You!

PRAYER JAR INSPIRATION:

My hope and joy rest in the God whose unfailing love surrounds me!

LEARNING THE SECRET

Always be full of joy in the Lord. I say it again—rejoice! . . .
I know how to live on almost nothing or with everything.
I have learned the secret of living in every situation, whether
it is with a full stomach or empty, with plenty or little.

PHILIPPIANS 4:4, 12 NLT

The Word tells us to rejoice in the Lord—and to do so always. Not just sometimes or some days. But all the time, every day!

Rejoicing always may take some focus, some intention from you. So, in those times when you are feeling as if your world is crumbling and tumbling down, do what others who have gone before you have done. Find a silver lining. Figure out how to rejoice in your situation no matter what you have lost or found. Teach yourself how to smile even when your heart is breaking.

This does not mean there will not be times when you need a good cry. It just means you are to make an effort to see the good in whatever circumstance you are facing. You are to rejoice in the Lord because He is with you wherever you are. And He will always be there to see you through.

Lord, teach me how to rejoice—always!

PRAYER JAR INSPIRATION:

I pray God will help me learn the secret of contentment—and rejoicing!

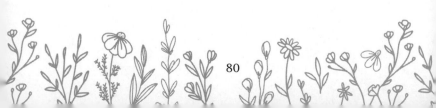

REJOICING IN ALL THINGS

Rejoice in hope; be patient in affliction; be persistent in prayer.

ROMANS 12:12 HCSB

Romans 12 gives us a list of all the things we're to do in this life in the body of Christ. Three very important to-dos appear in verse 12, where we're instructed to rejoice in hope, be patient during hardships, and pray continually.

To rejoice in hope, we must have great confidence in Christ, a knowledge deep within our hearts that He is with us, helping us, loving us, empowering us. Instead of turning tail at the first challenge, we must be patient and courageous, knowing Christ will lead us through whatever comes. But to have a hope we can rejoice in, to find that patience amid affliction, we must be praying continually, asking for His wisdom, guidance, and strength.

Today, find a way to have an ongoing conversation with Jesus—spoken or unspoken. And at the end of the day, take stock of where you are in hope and patience. Rejoice where God has brought you. And ask Him to help you do it all over again tomorrow. Chances are the more you practice, the more you'll be rejoicing in all things!

Help me, Lord, to rejoice in hope, be patient during hardship, and pray continually to You, the source and strength of my joy.

PRAYER JAR INSPIRATION:

Lord, help me to pray all day, to live from joy to joy.

MEETING FACE-TO-FACE

*Though I have many things to write to you, I don't want to
do so with paper and ink. Instead, I hope to be with you
and talk face to face so that our joy may be complete.*

2 JOHN 12 HCSB

Today there are so many different ways we can connect with each other. We can send texts and emails or make phone calls. We can put a post on social media or engage in a video call. We can even write letters by hand and send them via snail mail. But none of these things can ever take the place of actually meeting face-to-face.

We are social creatures. We need those personal interactions. When we are face-to-face, we are more focused, communicate easier, and can pick up on nonverbal cues. We can, if appropriate, hug and kiss each other, feel each other's presence.

Today, for complete joy, plan a safe face-to-face meeting with a loved one. And remember to keep meeting as a church family to encourage each other (Hebrews 10:25) in the name of Christ.

*Help me, Lord, to find a way to reach out to others with Your love
in my heart and Your message on my lips. In Jesus' name, amen.*

PRAYER JAR INSPIRATION:

My hope is to complete my joy by spending time with others.

HOPE
for Courage

Have you ever hoped for courage to face life's biggest challenges, not to mention the everyday struggles we have to deal with?

Webster's Dictionary says courage is the "mental or moral strength to venture, persevere and withstand danger, fear or difficulty." The New Testament word for courage (*tharsos*) can be translated as "confidence" or "boldness."

The greatest example of courage our world has ever known was when Jesus faced the ordeal of the cross. He knew what awaited Him, yet the Bible says in Luke 9:51 (KJV) that "he stedfastly set his face to go to Jerusalem." Because of His love for you and me, He was determined to go through with it so that those who called on His name would be saved.

We can take courage because God is always with us. We don't have to face the challenges of life alone. When we don't know what to do, He does. Jesus says in John 16:33 that we will have tribulation in this world. But we can "take heart" and "take courage" because Jesus is greater than the world. He has already overcome it for those He's redeemed. No matter what we are going through, we can be assured that it has not separated us from the love of God.

"Behold, God is my salvation; I will trust, and not be afraid: for the LORD JEHOVAH is my strength and my song; he also is become my salvation" (Isaiah 12:2 KJV).

BLESSED IN BELIEVING

"With God nothing [is or ever] shall be impossible."
Then Mary said, "Behold, I am the servant of the Lord;
may it be done to me according to your word."

LUKE 1:37–38 AMP

Mary was just a young girl when the angel Gabriel came to tell her she would be the most blessed of women. She had been chosen, favored by God, to conceive and give birth to a son she was to name Jesus.

Mary asked how this would happen since she was a virgin. The angel replied that the Holy Spirit would come upon her, and the resulting child would be called the Son of God.

Her response? "May it happen just like you said."

What courage this young girl had! And all because she believed in the God who does the impossible and keeps His word.

Later, Mary's cousin Elizabeth greeted her, saying, "Blessed. . . is she who believed and confidently trusted that there would be a fulfillment of the things that were spoken to her [by the angel sent] from the Lord" (Luke 1:45 AMP).

You too can take courage. Believe God's promises will become your reality. And you will be blessed in believing!

Lord, what You have promised will be realized in my life. In that I take courage, for with You walking beside me, nothing is impossible.

PRAYER JAR INSPIRATION:

I am blessed and emboldened by believing.

THE ROAD TAKEN

Barak said to her, "If you will go with me, I will go. But if you will not go with me, I will not go." "I will go with you," she said, "but you will receive no honor on the road you are about to take, because the Lord will sell Sisera into a woman's hand."

JUDGES 4:8–9 HCSB

Deborah was a woman, a prophet, a wife, and a judge of Israel. As she sat underneath a palm tree, the Israelites would come to her for judgment.

One day she called for Barak, a military commander of Israel. She told him that God wanted him to go to Mount Tabor with ten thousand men. There he would draw out Sisera, the general of the army of Jabin, a Canaanite king whose nine hundred chariots of iron were oppressing the people of Israel. And God would give Barak victory over Jabin's forces.

But Barak refused to go unless Deborah went with him.

Perhaps God is calling you to some face-off, but you hesitate because you are frightened, certain the other side will overwhelm you and your efforts.

Be like Deborah. Remember that your God is bigger than anything you're facing. And God will honor you on that road you take with Him.

Lord, give me the courage to step out in faith on the road You have placed before me.

PRAYER JAR INSPIRATION:

If I have faith and courage, God will deliver me!

BLESSED FOR BRAVERY

*Jael the wife of Heber took a tent peg, and took a hammer
in her hand. Then she went softly to him and drove the peg
into his temple until it went down into the ground while
he was lying fast asleep from weariness. So he died.*

JUDGES 4:21 ESV

Jael, like a lot of women, was identified merely as a wife of some man, in her case Heber. Yet because of her courage, she made a name for herself and God!

Barak's forces had put Sisera and his chariots on the run. Eventually, all the men in Sisera's army were defeated. . .except Sisera managed to flee on foot to the tent of his friend Heber the Kenite.

Jael, Heber's wife, greeted Sisera, inviting him to come into the tent. When he did, she covered him with a rug and gave him some water to drink. He asked her to keep his presence a secret. But when he fell asleep, Jael killed Sisera by driving a tent peg into his head.

Jael then found Barak, led him to her tent, and showed him the corpse of his enemy.

Woman of God, lean into the courage God offers you. Take hold of what's at hand. And you too can vanquish God's enemies.

Thank You, Lord, for giving me the tools to be courageous.

PRAYER JAR INSPIRATION:

God will bless my bravery in His name.

PASSING POWER ON

"Have I not commanded you? Be strong and courageous. Do not be frightened, and do not be dismayed, for the Lord your God is with you wherever you go." And Joshua commanded the officers of the people, "Pass through the midst of the camp and command the people, 'Prepare your provisions, for within three days you are to pass over this Jordan to go in to take possession of the land that the Lord your God is giving you to possess.'"

JOSHUA 1:9–11 ESV

After Moses died, God *commanded* Joshua to be strong and courageous. To not be afraid or dismayed. Because He would be with Joshua wherever he went, whatever he attempted for God.

Filled with the assurance of God's presence and power, Joshua commanded the leaders in charge of each tribe to tell the people to get ready. They were soon going to head into the Promised Land God had prepared for them.

God gives you all the power you need to do what He would have you do. Today He *commands* you to be strong and courageous. To not live in fear or be waylaid by panic. *Because God is with you wherever you go.*

Lord, today I take up Your command to be strong and courageous, assured You are with me wherever I go. In Jesus' name, amen.

PRAYER JAR INSPIRATION:

I need not live in fear. For God is with me wherever I go!

87

BEQUEATHED POWER

The king of Jericho sent word to Rahab and said, "Bring out the men who came to you and entered your house, for they came to investigate the entire land." But the woman had taken the two men and hidden them.

JOSHUA 2:3–4 HCSB

Before entering Jericho, Joshua sent some spies to scout the land. Those scouts ended up in the house of Rahab, the prostitute. But instead of turning them in, Rahab hid them from the king and his men. Later, convinced of God's great power, she was bold enough to make a deal with the Israelite spies: she would be silent if they would rescue her and her family when God's people invaded her town.

The spies agreed and rescued her as promised. Afterward, Rahab lived in Israel, married Salmon, and gave birth to a son named Boaz (Matthew 1:5), making her an ancestor of King David *and* Jesus.

You are a daughter of the Lord. To you God has bequeathed His power, a force that can melt the hearts and drain the courage of others (Joshua 2:11). Every day, believe in that power; take hold of it. Be as courageous as Rahab. Heaven only knows where doing so will lead you.

*Give me the courage, Lord, to take hold
of Your power and wield it as You see fit.*

PRAYER JAR INSPIRATION:

*Lord, my hope in Your power is deep, giving me
the courage to do what You call me to do.*

SUCH A TIME AS THIS

*"If you keep silent at this time, liberation and deliverance will
come to the Jewish people from another place, but you and
your father's house will be destroyed. Who knows, perhaps you
have come to your royal position for such a time as this."*

ESTHER 4:14 HCSB

Mordecai had discovered the evil plot of Haman, a nobleman in a high
position in King Xerxes's Persian kingdom. So Mordecai sent word to
his orphan cousin Esther, the beautiful Jewess that Xerxes had made
his queen. Mordecai urged her to speak to the king, proposing that
maybe she had become queen for such a time as this.

Esther knew that if she went to see the king before he invited her
into his presence, she might lose her head. Literally. Yet that's what
she decided she had to do. So, Esther asked Mordecai to have the
Jews fast and pray for her for three days and nights. Then she would
go to the king, and if she perished, she perished (Esther 4:16).

You too are here, in God's kingdom, for such a time as this. Ask
God to reveal your purpose. Then, shielded in prayer, take courage,
and do what He would have you do.

*Lord, I ask for the courage to do what You
have sent me to do—for such a time as this.*

PRAYER JAR INSPIRATION:

God will give me the courage to live out my purpose.

NOT KNOWING

*By faith Abraham, when he was called, obeyed and went
out to a place he was going to receive as an inheritance.
He went out, not knowing where he was going.*

HEBREWS 11:8 HCSB

God had told Abram to leave his home and his father's family and
head to a land that God would show him. There, God promised, He
would make Abram a great nation. He would bless him. He would
make his name great and make him a blessing.

Abram left what he knew to go to a place he knew not. . .all because God told him to do so. When was the last time you went to a
place without first checking a map or planning your route through
an app on your phone?

Blindly going where God would have you go, especially when
that place and the route to get there are unknown to you, takes a lot
of faith and courage. But if you ask, God will willingly give you an
abundance of both.

*I am ready, Lord, to go where You would have me go.
Please provide the faith and courage to get there from here.*

PRAYER JAR INSPIRATION:

*God is with me and will equip me with the
courage I need to travel into the unknown.*

MAKING A DIFFERENCE

God was good to the midwives. . . . And because the
midwives feared God, he gave them families of their own.

EXODUS 1:20–21 NLT

The Egyptian pharaoh, afraid of the number and strength of God's people, commanded they be made slaves. Yet "the more the Egyptians oppressed them, the more the Israelites multiplied and spread, and the more alarmed the Egyptians became" (Exodus 1:12 NLT). Finally, Pharaoh ordered Hebrew midwives Shiphrah and Puah to kill any boys born to the Israelites. But because the women feared God, they disobeyed the king's command.

When Pharaoh asked Shiphrah and Puah why they'd refused to follow his orders, they said about the Hebrew women, "They. . .have their babies so quickly that we cannot get there in time" (Exodus 1:19 NLT). So the Israelite population continued to grow. And God rewarded the midwives with families of their own.

When we respect and obey God's words, when we fear and revere Him more than anyone or anything else, God rewards us for our courage. This knowledge enables us to make a difference in God's eyes, no matter how humble our position is in man's eyes.

Lord, show me how I can make a difference
by following You above all others.

PRAYER JAR INSPIRATION:

My hope lies in the courage to do what is right in God's eyes.

FEARLESS IN FAITH

By faith Moses, after his birth, was hidden for three months by his
parents, because they saw he was a beautiful and divinely favored
child; and they were not afraid of the king's (Pharaoh's) decree.

HEBREWS 11:23 AMP

Pharaoh had commanded his people to drown all newborn male
Hebrew babies in the Nile. So when Amram's wife, Jochebed, gave
birth to their son Moses, they hid him for three months.

Then Jochebed came up with a bold plan. She made a basket from
reeds, covered it with tar and pitch, and put Moses in the small ark.
She then set it down in the reeds of the Nile. His sister, Miriam, stood
at a distance to see what would happen.

When Pharaoh's daughter came to the river, she saw the basket
and the Hebrew baby in it. Miriam asked if she wanted her to find
a Hebrew woman to nurse the infant. When the princess said yes,
Miriam came back with her mother, who was then paid by the princess
to nurse the child.

It's your faith that makes you fearless, giving you a steady mind to
come up with bold plans and the courage to follow through.

Grow my faith, Lord, so I can become a fearless follower,
living and working in Your will and Way.

PRAYER JAR INSPIRATION:

My faith gives me the calm to plan along with
the courage to see that plan through.

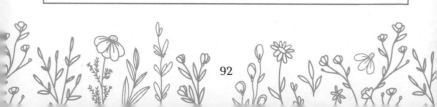

GIANT FEAR

"The land. . .is a land that devours its inhabitants. And all the people that we saw in it are men of great stature. There we saw the Nephilim (the sons of Anak are part of the Nephilim); and we were like grasshoppers in our own sight, and so we were in their sight."

NUMBERS 13:32–33 AMP

Moses sent twelve men to scout the Promised Land. When they returned, they admitted the land was beautiful and bountiful. The only problem was its inhabitants. Next to those giants, the scouts saw themselves as grasshoppers—and they must have seemed like grasshoppers in the eyes of the giants too!

Because of their fears, ten of the twelve spies not only refused to go into the Promised Land but begged Moses to let them go back to Egypt! Meanwhile, the other two spies, Caleb and Joshua, were willing to fight for the Promised Land, knowing God would be with them.

The ten spies' fear kept them wandering in the wilderness for the next forty years. Only Caleb and Joshua would live to enter the Promised Land.

Don't let fear belittle you and keep you from entering into the promises God has made. Instead, know God walks with you. And He's mightier than any giant you come across.

With You walking with me, Lord, I have no fear!

PRAYER JAR INSPIRATION:

My hope is in God, who's mightier than any giant I may encounter!

ENCOURAGED IN GOD

David was greatly distressed because the people spoke of stoning him,
for all of them were embittered, each man for his sons and daughters.
But David felt strengthened and encouraged in the Lord his God.

1 SAMUEL 30:6 AMP

When David and his men got home to Ziklag, they discovered that the Amalekites had not just burned their town but taken captive all the residents! Distraught because their wives and children had been kidnapped, David and his men "wept until they had no more strength to weep" (1 Samuel 30:4 ESV).

In their anguish, David's men began talking about stoning him. Meanwhile, "David found strength in the Lord his God" (1 Samuel 30:6 HCSB).

David then asked God if he should go after the Amalekites. And if he did, would he overtake them? The Lord told him, "Pursue them, for you will certainly overtake them and rescue the people" (1 Samuel 30:8 HCSB). David and his men followed God's advice and ended up bringing back not only all they'd lost but also plunder from those who had burned and raided their village!

When all seems lost, don't despair. Instead, strengthen and encourage yourself in the Lord. Ask Him for direction. And you'll recover what you've lost and more besides!

Help me, Lord, to look to You for all the courage and strength I need.

PRAYER JAR INSPIRATION:

God is the source of my strength and courage.

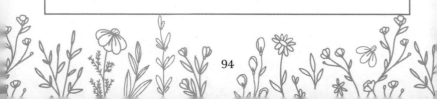

GOD'S GIRL

"Fear not, for I have redeemed you; I have called you by name, you are mine. When you pass through the waters, I will be with you; and through the rivers, they shall not overwhelm you; when you walk through fire you shall not be burned, and the flame shall not consume you."

ISAIAH 43:1–2 ESV

You are not your own. You are God's. He created you, formed you, saved you. And He, the Master of the universe, wants you to live a life without fear because He needs you to live out the purpose He made you for.

You *can* live without fear. How? By constantly and continually reminding yourself that when you pass through the waters, God will be in those waves with you. When you try to cross the flooded rivers, they won't overwhelm you because God is in the flood with you. And when you walk through fire, you'll not be burned nor consumed by the flames. Instead, you'll come out like Shadrach, Meshach, and Abednego—not only not singed but not even smelling of smoke!

To live without fear, constantly remember who you are and where God is. You are His precious daughter, and He is the omnipresent power that nothing and no one can conquer!

Help me, Lord, to continually remember that I am Your girl— and that You will be with me through flood and fire!

PRAYER JAR INSPIRATION:

My hope and courage are found in who God is!

A CERTAIN KIND
OF COURAGE

*In your hearts set Christ apart [as holy—acknowledging Him,
giving Him first place in your lives] as Lord. Always be ready
to give a [logical] defense to anyone who asks you to account
for the hope and confident assurance [elicited by faith] that
is within you, yet [do it] with gentleness and respect.*

1 Peter 3:15 amp

The Bible tells us time and time again that we're to make God our priority (Psalm 70:4); we're to seek Him first above all other things (Matthew 6:33). For in doing so, we will not only eliminate needless worry in our lives but find the happiness, peace, and courage we long for.

Equipped with that joy, calm, and courage, we will find a way to speak confidently to others about God. We'll find the right words to tell them—with gentleness and respect—what Jesus has done and continues to do in our lives.

Today, lean into the confidence that walking closely with God provides. Take a few minutes to write out what you might say to anyone who asks you about your church, the Word, or your faith. Then you will be numbered with the great host of "women who proclaim the good news" (Psalm 68:11 amp).

Help me, Lord, to make You number one in my life!

PRAYER JAR INSPIRATION:

*Making God a priority in my life is the first
step to spread the good news!*

YOUR INNER FIRE

Fan into flame the gracious gift of God, [that inner fire—the special endowment] which is in you. . . . For God did not give us a spirit of timidity or cowardice or fear, but [He has given us a spirit] of power and of love and of sound judgment and personal discipline [abilities that result in a calm, well-balanced mind and self-control].

2 TIMOTHY 1:6–7 AMP

When you first came to Christ, did you spend some time discovering your spiritual gift? Finding it most likely sparked your spiritual fire, so ready were you to serve God by using it to grow His kingdom. But, as the years went by, your initial spark may have died out.

It's time to fan back into a flame those embers of your gift so that you can serve God in a way no one else can. God equipped you with a unique talent. Use it, knowing that He has also given you the power, peace, love, and mind to do so.

Inspire me once more, Lord, to use the spiritual gift
You've blessed me with. Help me see it with new eyes.
Then give me the courage to use it in Your power!

PRAYER JAR INSPIRATION:

God of all gifts, thank You for giving me a
spirit of power, love, and self-discipline!

SEEKING COURAGE: PART 1

*Jehoshaphat was afraid and set himself [determinedly,
as his vital need] to seek the Lord. . . . "We are powerless
against this great multitude which is coming against us.
We do not know what to do, but our eyes are on You."*

2 CHRONICLES 20:3, 12 AMP

When King Jehoshaphat of Judah heard that a huge army was coming against him, he was filled with fear. So, he not only determined to seek the Lord but also proclaimed a fast throughout Judah. People came from all over the kingdom to "seek the LORD [longing for Him with all their heart]" (2 Chronicles 20:4 AMP).

Before his people, King Jehoshaphat explained to God the situation they faced. He humbly admitted they were powerless and had no idea what to do.

And God answered, speaking through the prophet Jahaziel: "Be not afraid or dismayed at this great multitude, for the battle is not yours, but God's" (2 Chronicles 20:15 AMP).

When fear strikes, stop. Admit you're powerless, not sure what to do. Then seek God with all your heart, knowing He *will* answer. He *will* stand with you.

*When fear knocks the wind out of me, Lord, remind me
that I am Your daughter. That if I set my heart to seek
Your face, You will answer me. You will be with me.*

PRAYER JAR INSPIRATION:

My eyes are on God, the One who gives me the courage to stand.

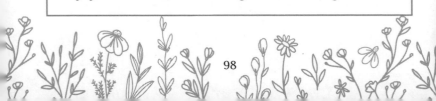

SEEKING COURAGE: PART 2

"You need not fight in this battle; take your positions, stand and witness the salvation of the LORD who is with you. . . . Do not fear or be dismayed; tomorrow go out against them, for the LORD is with you."

2 CHRONICLES 20:17 AMP

Once Jehoshaphat received an answer from the Lord, he bowed down with his face on the ground and worshipped Him.

The next day, Jehoshaphat followed God's detailed directions. He encouraged his people, saying, "Believe and trust in the LORD your God and you will be established (secure). Believe and trust in His prophets and succeed" (2 Chronicles 20:20 AMP).

Confident in God and His instructions, Jehoshaphat sent singers out before his army! And as soon as the singers began singing praises to God, the enemy armies attacked and destroyed each other. By the time King Jehoshaphat and his people got to the battlefield, all they had to do was collect all the plunder left behind—so much that it took them three days to gather!

Take heart! God will give you the courage to stand and follow His directions—no matter how bizarre they may seem—and will grant you victory.

Help me, Lord, to follow Your directions, knowing
I don't need to understand them to obey them.

PRAYER JAR INSPIRATION:

God, my hope lies in the wonder and glory of Your
immense power, grand plan, and awesome presence.

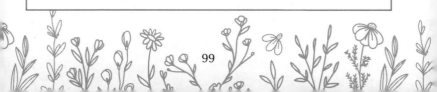

STICK-TO-ITIVENESS

David continued to address Solomon: "Take charge! Take heart!
Don't be anxious or get discouraged. God, my God, is with you in this;
he won't walk off and leave you in the lurch. He's at your side until
every last detail is completed for conducting the worship of God."

1 CHRONICLES 28:20 MSG

Young or old, we may at times lack the confidence and the courage to use the gifts God has given us. Perhaps we doubt whether we have the talent to do what we've been called to do. Or we imagine we'll run out of time to begin the project, much less complete it.

Yet, as Solomon was told and later discovered, whatever God has called us to do He will equip us to do—in both talent, resources, and time. So don't hesitate to begin the project God has tapped you for. And don't worry about having the time to complete it. Just continually seek God's direction, knowing He will be with you. He won't leave you in the lurch. He'll stick and stand with you till the end.

Help me focus on what You are doing in and through me,
Lord, instead of what I may lack. Give me the courage and
the faith to see a project through from beginning to end.

PRAYER JAR INSPIRATION:

God is my comfort and stay!

OVERCOME OR CONFIDENT?

Light shines in the darkness for the godly. They are generous,
compassionate, and righteous. . . . Such people will not be overcome
by evil. Those who are righteous will be long remembered. They do
not fear bad news; they confidently trust the LORD to care for them.

PSALM 112:4, 6–7 NLT

Naomi had lost her hope. Years ago, she, her husband, and her two
sons had left Bethlehem during a famine. They traveled to Moab,
where both sons found wives. But then her husband and sons died.
Crushed and brokenhearted, Naomi decided to go back home.

Naomi told her weeping daughters-in-law to return to their
mothers' houses, hoping each would find another husband. But one
of them, Ruth, insisted on going with Naomi, telling her, "Where you
go, I will go. Your God will be my God."

When the women entered Bethlehem, Naomi told those that
greeted her, "Do not call me Naomi ["pleasant"]; call me Mara ["bitter"],
for the Almighty has dealt very bitterly with me" (Ruth 1:20 ESV).
Little did she know how wondrously He would soon bless her life.

You can either allow yourself to be steamrolled by the trials of this
life or be confident God will take care of you. Which will you choose?

Help me, Lord, not to be overcome with trials but to be
filled with confidence that You will take care of me.

PRAYER JAR INSPIRATION:

I expect good things from God!

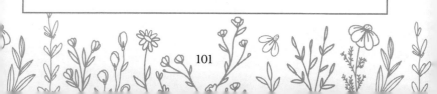

YAHWEH SUPREME

"Be strong and courageous! Don't be afraid or discouraged before
the king of Assyria or before the large army that is with him, for
there are more with us than with him. He has only human strength,
but we have Yahweh our God to help us and to fight our battles."

2 CHRONICLES 32:7–8 HCSB

Sennacherib, king of Assyria, had great plans. He intended to attack and conquer Judah. After all, he had a great army to help him do so.

But Hezekiah, king of Judah, had God on his side. And he reminded his people of that fact.

Sennacherib sent his servants to talk trash to the people of Judah. He asked them why they were trusting in Hezekiah during this siege of Jerusalem. Didn't they know how Sennacherib and his fathers had conquered many other lands? The gods of those lands couldn't save them, nor could Hezekiah's!

So the prophet Isaiah and Hezekiah prayed to God. And the Lord sent an angel to kill 185,000 Assyrians in one night. Afterward, Sennacherib returned to Assyria, where his sons killed him.

Take heart! No matter what you face, nothing is greater than your God.

Continually remind me, Lord, that I need not be
afraid, weak, or discouraged. For You are greater
than anything that could come against me!

PRAYER JAR INSPIRATION:

Yahweh is my strength, my courage, and my God!

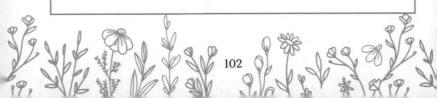

FOCUSED ON JESUS

"Yes, come," Jesus said. So Peter went over the side of the boat and walked on the water toward Jesus. But when he saw the strong wind and the waves, he was terrified and began to sink. "Save me, Lord!" he shouted. Jesus immediately reached out and grabbed him.

MATTHEW 14:29–31 NLT

After feeding the five thousand, Jesus had the disciples take the boat to the other side of the Sea of Galilee while He went up to a mountaintop to pray. When evening came, His followers found themselves in a storm with high winds and waves. So Jesus walked on the sea toward them, inadvertently terrifying them.

Jesus immediately reassured them, saying, "Take heart; it is I. Do not be afraid" (Matthew 14:27 ESV).

Peter said, "Lord, if it is you, command me to come to you on the water" (Matthew 14:28 ESV). So Jesus did.

Peter was actually walking on the water—until he took his eyes off Jesus. Then he began to sink in fear. He cried out for Jesus to save him, and He did.

When you take a big leap of faith, keep your eyes focused on Jesus. When you do, you won't notice the size and strength of lesser powers against you.

Jesus, my eyes are on You alone!

PRAYER JAR INSPIRATION:

My hope, confidence, and focus are on Jesus. He'll see me through!

NEVER ALONE

"Don't be afraid, for I am with you. Don't be discouraged, for I am your God. I will strengthen you and help you. I will hold you up with my victorious right hand. . . . For I hold you by your right hand—I, the Lord your God. And I say to you, 'Don't be afraid. I am here to help you.'"

ISAIAH 41:10, 13 NLT

No matter what others tell you, you are not alone in this world. God is with you wherever you go. His presence will strengthen you and help you. He will lift you out of pits of despair, pull your foot out of snares, and haul you out of the deep waters into which you are plunged. He is there beside you, continually telling you not to be afraid. You can turn to Him for whatever help, strength, rescuing, and empowerment you need, night or day.

It's this kind of knowledge that gave Joseph of Arimathea—"a respected member of the council, who was also himself looking for the kingdom of God" (Mark 15:43 ESV)—the courage, the boldness, to go to Pilate and ask for Jesus' body so he could prepare it for burial.

Daughter of God, sister of Christ, woman of the Holy Spirit, have courage. You never walk alone.

God, with You in my life, I will never fear.

PRAYER JAR INSPIRATION:

With God, I am never alone.

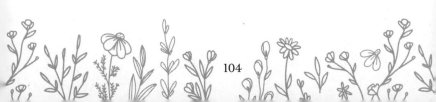

HOPE
for Calm

Have you ever been caught in the middle of a storm either on land or out on the water someplace? Were you frightened and hoping for the weather to calm so you could feel safe and have a sense of peace?

Sometimes the storms we encounter in everyday life turn our world upside down. Have your nerves ever felt frazzled and you hoped for calm but couldn't seem to find a way to relax or let go of your fears?

The Bible has a solution for fear. When I've been in the midst of chaos and felt fearful and hopeless, reflecting on this verse has always calmed my fears and helped me relax and feel hopeful: "Be still, and know that I am God" (Psalm 46:10 KJV). Another good verse that reminds me to remain calm is "Humble yourselves. . .under the mighty hand of God, that he may exalt you in due time: casting all your care upon him; for he careth for you" (1 Peter 5:6–7 KJV).

Doubt is the opposite of faith and hope. When it seems that there's nothing left and fears abound, there is hope for calm when we put our faith and trust in Jesus.

"ALL IS WELL"

She called to her husband and said, "Send me one of the servants
and one of the donkeys, that I may quickly go to the man of God
and come back again." And he said, "Why will you go to him today?
It is neither new moon nor Sabbath." She said, "All is well."

2 KINGS 4:22–23 ESV

A prominent Shunammite woman talked her husband into making a room in their home for the prophet Elisha. In return, Elisha told her she would hold a son in her arms by the next year.

And it happened just as Elisha said.

Years later, the Shunammite's son fell ill and died in his mother's arms. So, she took her child up to Elisha's room, gently laid him on the prophet's bed, then told her husband she was going to see the man of God. When he asked why, she simply responded with "All is well."

She said the same thing to Elisha's servant. And when she reached Elisha himself, she explained all. Later, he brought the child back to life and placed him in his mother's arms once again.

When you trust God, you can have peace knowing that no matter what's happening in your life, all is truly well.

Lord, in You I trust. With You, I know all is and will be well.

PRAYER JAR INSPIRATION:

I live in the hope that no matter what's
happening in my life, all is truly well.

PEACEMAKERS

David said to Abigail, "Praise to the Lord God of Israel, who
sent you to meet me today! Your discernment is blessed,
and you are blessed. Today you kept me from participating
in bloodshed and avenging myself by my own hand."

1 Samuel 25:32–33 hcsb

While in the wilderness with his fighting men, David guarded the rich man Nabal's sheep. Later, David asked Nabal for some provisions for his men and himself. But Nabal abruptly and rudely refused David's request.

One of Nabal's servants ran to tell Abigail, Nabal's wife. To keep the peace, she had her servants load up some donkeys and take them to David and his men. She would soon follow.

Abigail's actions saved not just herself but her household needless bloodshed. For David accepted her apology and her wisdom.

When Abigail returned home to a drunken Nabal, she waited until the next day to let him know what she'd done. And when she did, he had a stroke. Nabal died ten days later. Sometime after that, David took Abigail to wife.

Be as Abigail, a maker and maintainer of peace (Matthew 5:9). And you too will find yourself more than blessed.

Help me stay spiritually calm, Lord,
so that I can be one of Your peacemakers.

PRAYER JAR INSPIRATION:

Grow my faith, Lord, so that I can trust You more. . .and in
trusting, stay calm. . .and in staying calm, find a peaceful path.

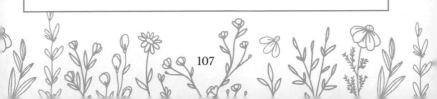

PURSUING PEACE

What man is there who desires life and loves many days, that he may see good? Keep your tongue from evil and your lips from speaking deceit. Turn away from evil and do good; seek peace and pursue it. The eyes of the LORD are toward the righteous and his ears toward their cry.

PSALM 34:12–15 ESV

It's good to promote peace. But God wants you to go beyond that. God wants you to *pursue* peace! To go after it any way and any day you can! Why? Because that's one way to shed His light in this world.

One approach to pursuing peace is to make sure that what you say helps, not hinders, the hearer. Say things that are encouraging, that build others up. Another approach is to turn away from evil, to eschew it. Instead, do good.

Throughout His Word, God makes it clear that He has His eyes focused on those who are doing the right thing—reverencing Him, obeying His commandment to love Him and others. It's the prayers of those who are following Him that He hears and responds to.

Woman of God, what can—what will—you do to pursue peace today?

Show me, Lord, how I can promote and pursue peace today.

PRAYER JAR INSPIRATION:

What the world needs now is love and peace.
Help me, Lord, to be a promoter and pursuer of both.

A GREAT CALM

*He got up and [sternly] rebuked the wind and said to the sea, "Hush,
be still (muzzled)!" And the wind died down [as if it had grown weary]
and there was [at once] a great calm [a perfect peacefulness].*

MARK 4:39 AMP

One evening, Jesus and His followers left the crowds and headed in
boats to the other side of the Sea of Galilee. When a fierce wind-
storm began to rage, waves started breaking over the boat so that it
quickly became swamped.

The disciples woke Jesus, who had fallen asleep in the stern, and
said, "Teacher, do you not care that we are perishing?" (Mark 4:38
ESV). Now wide awake, Jesus "rebuked the wind and said to the sea,
'Peace! Be still!' And the wind ceased, and there was a great calm"
(Mark 4:39 ESV).

As a daughter of God, chances are good you'll face a number of
seemingly unrelenting squalls in your life. Yet there's no need to panic.
You're voyaging with Jesus! The entire earth was made through Him,
and He has the power to calm not only nature but also your fears. So
the next time you feel a squall coming on, turn to Jesus. Repeat to
yourself His own words: "Peace! Be still." Then wait for a great calm
to settle on you.

Jesus, calm me as only You can.

PRAYER JAR INSPIRATION:

I find peace in the knowledge of Jesus' power.

DO WHAT YOU CAN

Jesus said, "Leave her alone. Why are you bothering her? She has done a noble thing for Me. . . . She has done what she could; she has anointed My body in advance for burial. I assure you: Wherever the gospel is proclaimed in the whole world, what this woman has done will also be told in memory of her."

MARK 14:6, 8–9 HCSB

While Jesus was dining at the table of Simon the leper, a woman came in with a jar of expensive perfume. She broke the jar then poured the ointment over His head.

Some who were present admonished her, wondering why she'd been allowed to waste such expensive perfume when the money from selling it would have been better spent on the poor. But Jesus scolded them, telling them to leave her alone, for His followers would always have the poor with them. They could help them however they wanted when He was gone. But this woman had done what she could to prepare Him for His upcoming burial.

Let's do what is in our heart, power, ability, and budget to do for God. And He will commend us for it.

Remind me each day, Lord, to do what good I can—and to leave the rest of the world's problems and burdens in Your capable hands.

PRAYER JAR INSPIRATION:

I need not be a superwoman. All I need to do is focus on being a godly woman.

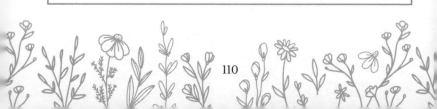

110

FROM CHAOS TO CALM

*Why are you in despair, O my soul? And why are you restless and
disturbed within me? Hope in God and wait expectantly for Him, for I
shall again praise Him, the help of my [sad] countenance and my God.*

PSALM 43:5 AMP

When ungodly people are unjustly attacking you, you might find
yourself on the verge of losing your peace. So take a time-out to remind yourself of who God is—your strength, a stronghold in whom
you can take refuge (Psalm 43:2).

Ask God for direction, for help in staying calm. Ask Him to shine
His light and truth on your path so that you can find your way back
into His presence, a place where you can bend your knee in humility
before Him, find a fountain of joy, and begin to praise instead of
panic (Psalm 43:3–4). Lastly, speak to your soul, bringing it back to
a place of hope, of expectation of God's shelter, love, and calm. Ask
your innermost self, *Why should you be upset when you can abide in Him?*
For in God lies your hope of future praise!

*God, help me regain my peace. Remind me that You are my
strength and my God of hope and joy! In Jesus' name, amen.*

PRAYER JAR INSPIRATION:

*God reigns within, guiding me out of the
world's chaos and ushering me into His calm.*

REMAIN CALM

"Do not be afraid! Take your stand [be firm and confident and undismayed] and see the salvation of the LORD which He will accomplish for you today; for those Egyptians whom you have seen today, you will never see again. The LORD will fight for you while you [only need to] keep silent and remain calm."

EXODUS 14:13–14 AMP

When you're between a rock and a hard place, it's hard to stand still, to be calm, to keep your peace. But it is possible—just ask the Israelites.

The Egyptians with their chariots had come after the Israelites. The Israelites were trapped between an infuriated army and the Red Sea. Panicked, they cried out to God. Then they complained to Moses, asking why he'd brought them out here in the wilderness to be killed when they could've just stayed in Egypt and died there.

So Moses reassured them, telling them not to be afraid but to stand firm. They would soon witness the Lord saving them from their peril. He assured them that the enemy they saw today they'd never see again. All they had to do was remain calm and watch.

God is telling you the same thing today. Don't panic. He's got this battle. Just remain calm and watch.

Lord of my salvation, help me remain calm, cool, and collected in You.

PRAYER JAR INSPIRATION:

Because God is in control, I aim to stay calm.

112

EVERLASTING ARMS

There is none like the God of Jeshurun, who rides the heavens to your aid, the clouds in His majesty. The God of old is your dwelling place, and underneath are the everlasting arms. He drives out the enemy before you. . . . He is the shield that protects you, the sword you boast in.

DEUTERONOMY 33:26–27, 29 HCSB

Other people may have power, wealth, and false gods, but you have the God of Jeshurun. And there is no one and nothing like Him. He is the One who actually rides the heavens to reach you, to help you. He is your Rock, your Refuge, your Dwelling Place. And underneath are His almighty arms that are ready to catch you, protect you, lift you, comfort you.

This God unlike any other will drive your enemy away from you. He is the shield of protection that encases you and the sword that fights for you.

Knowing that you have this God—a Being of immense power, an eternal safety net to catch you, arms ready, willing, and able to hold you—in your life should and can fill you with an overwhelming sense of calm. All you need to do is look upward, look inward. He is there for you—and always will be.

Lord, there is none like You! Help me keep myself in You, my Rock, my Refuge, my Protection.

PRAYER JAR INSPIRATION:

I live within reach of God—the One with everlasting arms!

CONSTANT PEACE

"You will keep in perfect and constant peace the one whose mind is steadfast [that is, committed and focused on You—in both inclination and character], because he trusts and takes refuge in You [with hope and confident expectation]."

Isaiah 26:3 AMP

A million things could go wrong during a day: you could get a flat tire on the way home from the grocery store; the clothes dryer could break down, leaving you with sopping wet sheets; you could get a call from the school nurse to pick up your child in the middle of a workday; your husband could ask for a divorce; or you could get a diagnosis of cancer. From day to day, hour to hour, minute to minute, you don't know what may or may not happen. So many things are out of your control.

Yet you can still have peace. How? By keeping your thoughts focused on God. By trusting in Him and taking shelter in Him. By confidently knowing that no matter what happens, He will bring out something good in the worst of circumstances.

Show me how to keep my mind on You, Lord, to run to You for refuge, trusting You to bring the best out of any situation. For I want, I need, I long for constant peace in You.

PRAYER JAR INSPIRATION:

Today I will trust and focus on God, my Fortress, Shield, and bringer of good.

RETURNING TO GOD

The Lord God, the Holy One of Israel has said this,
"In returning [to Me] and rest you shall be saved,
in quietness and confident trust is your strength."

ISAIAH 30:15 AMP

In Isaiah 30, God warned the people of Judah not to make an alliance with Egypt. He said they'd be sorry if they carried out a plan that was not His. . .if they made an alliance but not one of His Spirit. . .if they went down to Egypt without talking to Him about it first. . .if they took refuge in Pharaoh's stronghold, not in Him.

God wants His people to stop turning to others for help. He is longing to be gracious to them, to have compassion on them, to bless them.

When your peace has flown from your mind, your heart, your situation, your circumstances, take stock of where you are. Then do whatever you need to do to return to God. For there you will find not just Him but rest and rescuing. In Him, you will find quietness and confidence, peace and blessings, love and compassion, guidance and grace.

My peace has flown, Lord. Grant me peace as I return
to You for rest and rescue. Help me regain my strength
in quietness and confident trust in You.

PRAYER JAR INSPIRATION:

My hope of shelter, guidance, rest, salvation,
and peace lies in my returning to God!

CARED FOR AND CARRIED

"Listen to me. . . . I have cared for you since you were born. Yes, I carried you before you were born. I will be your God throughout your lifetime—until your hair is white with age. I made you, and I will care for you. I will carry you along and save you."

You may not always have your parents with you. But you will always have Father God.

God has carried and cared for you not only since you were born. He's done so *before* you entered this worldly realm! And He will continue to carry and care for you even when your hair starts to turn gray then white with age.

Why? Because He loves you. He loves spending time with you. He made you to be in a relationship with Him. He loves to see you live out the purpose He created you for. Like any father, He is a proud Papa.

So don't worry about the past, present, or future. He'll be with you through it all, beaming His light, love, and protection on your path. Your job? Enjoy the ride!

I find great peace in knowing, Lord, that You have been and always will be caring for and carrying me! What a wonderful Savior!

PRAYER JAR INSPIRATION:

*God is my constant caretaker and carrier.
I rest easy in that knowledge!*

LORD OF LOVE

"Do not let your hands fall limp. The LORD your God is in your midst, a Warrior who saves. He will rejoice over you with joy; He will be quiet in His love [making no mention of your past sins], He will rejoice over you with shouts of joy."

ZEPHANIAH 3:16–17 AMP

Peace can be difficult to obtain when your mind ruminates on all the things you have done wrong in the past—all the misdeeds you cannot undo, the words you cannot take back. When your mind is fixated on such things, it's hard to move forward, to turn to God, to live the life He created you to live.

Take heart, woman of God. For He is with you, in your midst. He is a mighty Warrior who is ready to save you. All He wants to do is love you and do so without bringing up all that you have done wrong. He will not harp on all the ways you have messed up. Instead, He will rejoice over you with songs and shouts of joy.

Change the picture of God in your mind from a stern taskmaster to a loving Lord. Then rejoice with Him as you regain your peace and the strength you need to serve Him.

Thank You, Lord, for substituting my shame with Your peace.

PRAYER JAR INSPIRATION:

My hope of peace lies in my vision of a loving Lord!

NEVER FORGOTTEN

*"Can a woman forget her nursing child, or lack compassion for
the child of her womb? Even if these forget, yet I will not forget
you. Look, I have inscribed you on the palms of My hands."*

ISAIAH 49:15–16 HCSB

There may be times when you feel a bit lost in this world, like everyone
has forgotten you, like no one understands you or has compassion for you.

But God wants you to know the truth. He wants you to look
beyond the misgivings that have beleaguered you, the thoughts that
have led you down a false path.

Your God is like a woman nursing her child. Although the umbilical cord has been cut, she automatically responds to her child's
needs, gushing milk from her breasts at the first sound of her child's
cry. Yet even if a good mother would forget her child, God wouldn't.
Ever. God has gone so far as to engrave a picture of you on the palms
of His mighty hands. Your portrait is forever in His presence. Why
not make sure He is continually in yours? In doing so, you will find
the calm you crave.

*Knowing You will never forget me or ever lack
compassion for me, Lord, fills my heart with joy
and my spirit with ease. All praise to Your name!*

PRAYER JAR INSPIRATION:

*In God's eyes, I will never be forgotten or forsaken.
Ah, Lord, what love You have, what peace I claim!*

FINDING REST

"Come to Me, all who are weary and heavily burdened [by religious rituals that provide no peace], and I will give you rest [refreshing your souls with salvation]. Take My yoke upon you and learn from Me [following Me as My disciple], for I am gentle and humble in heart, and you will find rest (renewal, blessed quiet) for your souls."

<small>MATTHEW 11:28–29 AMP</small>

Jesus provides a simple pathway to realizing His peace. All you need to do is come to Him and lay down your burdens. He'll give you the rest you need if you're burned out on religion. He'll refresh you from the weariness you have suffered by wending your way through this world.

With Jesus, you will be able to recover your true life, one that entails simply following Him. And in doing so, you'll not only find the peace you pine for but "learn the unforced rhythms of grace." As you endeavor to keep company with Him, "you'll learn to live freely and lightly" a life worth living (Matthew 11:29–30 MSG).

I come to You, Lord, ready to lay down my
burdens and pick up Your peace and grace.

PRAYER JAR INSPIRATION:

In Jesus, I live and hope to "learn the unforced
rhythms of grace" (Matthew 11:29 MSG).

FAITHFUL LOVE

"The mountains may move and the hills disappear, but even then my faithful love for you will remain. My covenant of blessing will never be broken," says the LORD, who has mercy on you. . . . "No weapon turned against you will succeed. . . . These benefits are enjoyed by the servants of the LORD."

ISAIAH 54:10, 17 NLT

When everything—including all that surrounds you—seems as if it's falling apart, one thing will never end or change. And that's the faithful love God has for you.

God's promise of blessing on you will never be broken. Even if mountains shake and hills fall away, His love will remain. And no matter how far you look into the future, no weapon that's turned against you will prevail. This is what the woman who lives and walks in His Way can count on.

With and in God, you can find the calm you need amid global warming, natural disasters, famine, drought, political unrest, and war. For the Lord loves those who serve Him, and He will do anything to protect those who live to love Him and further His kingdom.

Thank You, Lord, for reminding me that no matter how fouled up things may become on this earth, You continue to love me and have mercy on me. How may I serve You today?

PRAYER JAR INSPIRATION:

God's faithfulness in love and protection gives me coveted calm.

JESUS' PEACE

"Peace I leave with you; My [perfect] peace I give to you; not as the world gives do I give to you. Do not let your heart be troubled, nor let it be afraid. [Let My perfect peace calm you in every circumstance and give you courage and strength for every challenge.]"

JOHN 14:27 AMP

When an angel appeared to announce Jesus' birth to simple shepherds, his first words to them were "Don't be afraid" (Luke 2:10 HCSB). Good news that would bring great joy had entered the worldly realm. Immediately after the angel's announcement, the heavenly host joined him, proclaiming glory to God and peace on earth.

When Jesus told His followers He would be leaving soon, He began with "Your heart must not be troubled" and "Peace I leave with you" (John 14:1, 27 HCSB). Then, having risen from the dead, Jesus greeted His followers with the words "Peace to you!" (John 20:19 HCSB).

Daughter of God, Jesus has left you His peace for the asking, taking, and sharing. The peace He offers you, the peace within your reach, is one that will enable you to be calm in every situation; it will give you strength for every challenge.

Take the peace offered. And become even more like your Savior.

Bless me, Lord, with Your peace.

PRAYER JAR INSPIRATION:

My hope lies in the peace Jesus brought and spread, from His beginning to His never ending.

BE STILL

"Be still and know (recognize, understand) that I am God.
I will be exalted among the nations! I will be exalted in
the earth." The LORD of hosts is with us; the God of Jacob
is our stronghold [our refuge, our high tower].

PSALM 46:10–11 AMP

When your world has been shaken up, when you see no way out of your troubles, when you feel friendless and fearful, be still. Take a few deep breaths. And settle your mind on God.

See the Lord as your Refuge, Strength, and Helper. Remind yourself that you need not fear anything because He has you in the palm of His hand. So even if the earth quakes and the mountains topple into the sea, even though the waters may roar and foam, you have someone on your side: the Creator, Sustainer, and Maintainer of the universe.

God will never let you down, never allow you to falter. Jesus walks beside you, before you, behind you, and the Spirit resides within you.

And you don't need to wait until trouble comes to be still in God. Make it an everyday practice. Then when times get really tough, you'll know the best route to capturing His calm.

Help me, Lord, to be still and know You are with me.

PRAYER JAR INSPIRATION:

I find God in the stillness of my soul,
the calm of my heart, the peace of my spirit.

INNER CALM

*Let the peace of Christ [the inner calm of one who walks daily
with Him] be the controlling factor in your hearts [deciding
and settling questions that arise]. To this peace indeed you
were called as members in one body [of believers].*

COLOSSIANS 3:15 AMP

Colossians 3:15 says we're to let the peace of Christ—the inner calm of the woman who walks with Him every day—rule in our hearts. But to understand that peace, we must understand the Man who embodied it.

No matter how large the crowds, how stubborn the unbelievers, how dense the disciples, how unkind the religious leaders, how needy the people, or how little the time, Jesus kept His peace by tapping into the power of His Papa.

To grasp that peace of Christ—to know it, to understand it, to claim it—we must spend some time each day in the New Testament accounts of Jesus. We must tap into the calm we uncover there. We must allow it to rule our hearts and settle any questions that have arisen. We must permit it to direct our lives. For it is to this peace of Christ that we as women of the Way have been called.

Help me, Lord, to understand and tap into the calm of Christ.

PRAYER JAR INSPIRATION:

*My hope of peace lies in grasping and
making mine the inner calm of Christ.*

FIXED THOUGHTS

Fix your thoughts on what is true, and honorable, and right, and pure, and lovely, and admirable. Think about things that are excellent and worthy of praise. Keep putting into practice all you learned and received from me—everything you heard from me and saw me doing. Then the God of peace will be with you.

PHILIPPIANS 4:8–9 NLT

When our minds are fixed on bad news, it's easy to get depressed, feel hopeless, and lose our peace. That's why God's Word encourages us to fix our thoughts on things that are true, noble, authentic, pure, and lovely. Things that we can stand up and cheer about.

Fixing our thoughts on good things may mean turning away from social media or news outlets that are looking more for a high number of readers than truth. It may mean not streaming a program that's filled with violence and instead watching one that raises our spirits or fills us with awe.

Today, start making a conscious effort to feed yourself only those things that meet the requirements of Philippians 4:8–9. Try doing so for a week or two, taking note of whatever changes occur. See how fixing your thoughts on what's good brings you closer to the peace of God.

Lord, remind me to keep my thoughts fixed on the good. Lead me to Your peace.

PRAYER JAR INSPIRATION:

Today my mind is looking for good!

HOPE
for Good

Have you ever had days when you felt overwhelmed by troubled circumstances, and you prayed that something good would happen? It's a normal reaction for us to hope for better days. We want good health, blessings from above, and miracles to take place.

Why should we have hope for good? Because God Himself is good, He wants us to have better things either in this life or the next. "And we know that in all things God works for the good of those who love him, who have been called according to his purpose" (Romans 8:28 NIV).

How do we develop a hope for good? We rely on God's presence. When we go through difficult times, God can use them to shape us into the image of Jesus. We rely on God's provision. He wants us to realize that His grace is sufficient. And we rely on God's mighty power. When we are weak and feel hopeless, if we turn to God, His power will rest on us. Is your hope for good faltering? Remember to put your hope in His presence, His provision, and His power.

ENDLESS GOOD

Don't be afraid, O land. Be glad now and rejoice, for the Lord has done great things. Don't be afraid, you animals of the field, for the wilderness pastures will soon be green. The trees will again be filled with fruit; fig trees and grapevines will be loaded down once more. Rejoice, you people of Jerusalem! Rejoice in the Lord your God! For the rain he sends demonstrates his faithfulness. Once more the autumn rains will come, as well as the rains of spring.

JOEL 2:21–23 NLT

There will be days when hope seems to have deserted us and we cannot remember the ways God has done so much good. That's our cue to go outside, revel in nature, bathe ourselves in the forests, look up into the starry night, and remind ourselves how God continues to bring good things into our lives, sometimes without us even asking for them.

Preacher and author George MacDonald wrote, "We walk without fear, full of hope and courage and strength to do His will, waiting for the endless good which He is always giving as fast as He can get us able to take it in."

Today, look for and take joy in the good things God is bringing your way!

May all nature rejoice with me, Lord,
as I revel in You and Your goodness to me!

PRAYER JAR INSPIRATION:

My hope is revived by God's endless good!

RAY OF HOPE

*Oh, how abundant is your goodness, which you have stored up for
those who fear you and worked for those who take refuge in you!*

PSALM 31:19 ESV

When you can't take the world's woes anymore, when nothing seems
to lift your lips into a smile, you can still uncover a significant ray of
hope in God. But first you must turn away from the endless bad news
and turn to God. Ask Him to help you focus on the good things that
are coming your way, those He has stored up for you, the wonders
that you cannot even begin to imagine.

Do what Jesus did—the One who has by example already shown
you the way: entrust your spirit into God's hands (Psalm 31:5). He will
pull your foot out of the trap you are ensnared in (Psalm 31:4–5). He
will rescue you from the negative thoughts pressing into your mind.

Woman of God's Way, trust that He will come through for you.
"Be strong, and let your heart take courage, all you who wait for the
LORD!" (Psalm 31:24 ESV).

> *"I trust in you, O LORD. . . . My times are in your hand. . . .*
> *Blessed be the LORD, for he has wondrously shown*
> *his steadfast love to me" (Psalm 31:14–15, 21 ESV).*

PRAYER JAR INSPIRATION:

*Shine Your rays of goodness on my path,
Lord, so I may once more breathe hope.*

SOWING GOOD

Don't be deceived: God is not mocked. For whatever a man sows he will also reap. . . . So we must not get tired of doing good, for we will reap at the proper time if we don't give up.

GALATIANS 6:7, 9 HCSB

Every moment of your life, you have the choice to sow either good or bad. And whatever it is that you sow, that is what you will also reap.

So how do you sow good? You follow the promptings of the Spirit. When the Spirit hints that you should donate to a shelter or work at a food pantry, you follow that hint. When the Spirit prompts you to take a tin of cookies to an elderly neighbor, you start gathering the ingredients. When the Spirit urges you to do a pledge walk, you begin finding some sponsors and check out the tread on your sneakers.

And no matter how well or not so well your work at the pantry or your cookie baking or your walk goes, take it in stride and just keep doing good. For in doing that, you will someday reap an amazing harvest for God!

Spirit, show me what good works I can do!

PRAYER JAR INSPIRATION:

May I not only spread good but increase others' hope!

GOD'S GOOD

"I am Joseph your brother, whom you sold into Egypt. Now do not be distressed or angry with yourselves because you sold me here, for God sent me ahead of you to save life and preserve our family."

GENESIS 45:4–5 AMP

Joseph experienced many hardships beginning on the day his jealous older brothers threw him into a pit. Afterward, they sold him to traveling traders, who in turn sold him to an Egyptian officer to serve as a slave in his home. That same officer's wife later accused Joseph of attempted rape, after which an innocent Joseph was thrown into a dungeon. There he successfully interpreted the dreams of the king's baker and wine bearer, but upon his release, the latter soon forgot about Joseph—until the king himself needed dreams interpreted.

The point is, no matter what happened to Joseph, he never complained to God. Instead, the Lord was with him, and so would bless him, making Joseph a successful man (Genesis 39:2–3, 5, 21, 23) even amid what seemed to be dire straits.

This story is a good reminder that when others intend evil against God's children, we can be assured He will turn that evil into something good. Why? Because when we stick with God, He sticks with us, blessing us even in times of trial.

Regardless of what comes my way, Lord,
I'm sticking with You, the God of good!

PRAYER JAR INSPIRATION:

God will turn all evil against me into good!

GOOD BREEDS KINDNESS

"You planned evil against me; God planned it for good to bring about the present result—the survival of many people. Therefore don't be afraid. I will take care of you and your little ones." And he comforted them and spoke kindly to them.

GENESIS 50:20–21 HCSB

Joseph understood that because he'd not lost faith in God—but grew even closer to Him amid his ordeals—God turned the evil that had been done to him into good for himself and for others! Because of this knowledge, Joseph had no desire to seek revenge for what his brothers had done to him—even though his brothers' actions meant Joseph had to go without the love and affection of his earthly father for many years. Even then, Joseph determined not only to forgive his brothers and their families but also to be kind to them after his father's death.

Today, consider those who have wronged you. Consider how God already has or sometime will turn that evil into something good. Then resolve not only to forgive the wrongdoers but also to show them kindness, just as God has done for you.

God, turn all evil done against me into good. Then help me forgive and treat gently those who have done me wrong.

PRAYER JAR INSPIRATION:

Only God can turn evil into good, cruelty into kindness.

FINDING GOOD

*He who pays attention to the word [of God] will find
good, and blessed (happy, prosperous, to be admired)
is he who trusts [confidently] in the Lord.*

PROVERBS 16:20 AMP

God doesn't want you to be just a reader of His Word. He wants you to pay attention to it—to follow through on what it tells you to do and who it tells you to be. For when you really sink your heart, mind, body, soul, and spirit into what God through His Word is instructing you to do and be, you see yourself, the world, and your place in it with new eyes.

Make it a point each day not just to read a bit of the Bible and a short devotion but also to study His Word. Take one passage, one verse, one phrase and meditate on it. Chew on it. Then spend the day and night digesting it, asking God what He wants you to learn and then do with this information. Trust that He will bring scripture's meaning to life and into your life. In doing so, you will find His good surrounding you.

*Help me, Lord, to be not just a woman of the Way but a woman
of Your Word. Tell me what You would have me know. Then
reveal to me the good, the blessings sparkling all around me.*

PRAYER JAR INSPIRATION:

*My hope is to see God's blessings to me
through the lens of His good Word.*

WOMAN AT WORK

By grace you have been saved through faith. And this is not your own doing; it is the gift of God, not a result of works, so that no one may boast. For we are his workmanship, created in Christ Jesus for good works, which God prepared beforehand, that we should walk in them.

EPHESIANS 2:8–10 ESV

God has showered His grace on you. Not because of anything you've done, but because He loves you and has a plan for your life.

You, God's masterpiece in Christ, have been designed to do good works—ones that He prepared long ago, way ahead of time, so that you would walk in them, perform them.

Today and every day, live with that intention. Keep your eyes on where God is working around you. Seek what He would have you get involved in.

And don't worry that you may not be ready or have the time to do what you've been called to do. Instead, remember that God will prepare you for whatever needs your doing. . .in His time.

Thank You, Lord, for designing me and equipping me for the work You have in mind for me. My sleeves are rolled up. I'm ready to go. Now, Lord, reveal what You would have me do—for You!

PRAYER JAR INSPIRATION:

Make me, Lord, a woman at work for Your good!

CONQUERING EVIL

Never return evil for evil or insult for insult [avoid scolding, berating, and any kind of abuse], but on the contrary, give a blessing [pray for one another's well-being, contentment, and protection]; for you have been called for this very purpose, that you might inherit a blessing [from God that brings well-being, happiness, and protection].

I PETER 3:9 AMP

Wondering why you've not had a lot of good, an abundance of blessings, come your way? Perhaps it's because you're giving back what you get.

Many people find it easy to slap back when they're slapped, to insult when they're insulted, to pay back evil for evil. But God wants us to do the complete opposite. Although it goes against our automatic reflexes, God wants us to pay back evil with good (Romans 12:21). Why? Because that's what Jesus did.

After so much evilness had come upon Him—after He'd been harassed, threatened, deserted, beaten, denuded, and crucified—Jesus did an amazing thing. *He died for us! Even before we knew Him!* Jesus was good to us when we were evil, and God wants you to go and do the same.

Lord, to be like Jesus, I too must find a way to conquer evil with good. So the next time I'm yelled at, reviled, insulted, and abused, give me the strength to return that evil with a blessing. In Jesus' name. Amen.

PRAYER JAR INSPIRATION:

Lord, help me join You in conquering evil.

LONGED-FOR GOOD

*They cried to the LORD in their trouble, and he delivered them
from their distress. He made the storm be still, and the waves
of the sea were hushed. Then they were glad that the waters
were quiet, and he brought them to their desired haven.*

PSALM 107:28–30 ESV

When we're in trouble, God will surely help us. But how can He do so if we do not ask?

It's not that God doesn't know what's happening in our lives. It's that He wants us to come to Him, to tell Him all that's on our minds, to ask for His help, to allow ourselves to conclude that *He* is God, not we. Our good comes from His hands, not our own.

Too often, we don't pray because we think we can get ourselves out of the jam we're in. But then, as we get more and more desperate, we finally pray—to our relief and God's pleasure—and find the good we've longed for come on the wings of heaven.

Today, consider what you've been holding back from God. Explain the situation and your feelings. Ask for His help. And before you know it, He'll calm the storm you've been riding through and bring you to where you desire to be.

Lord, I need Your help. . . .

PRAYER JAR INSPIRATION:

God has good awaiting me. It's time to ask.

<u>DARE</u> TO HOPE

It is because of the LORD's lovingkindnesses that we are not
consumed, because His [tender] compassions never fail. They are
new every morning; great and beyond measure is Your faithfulness.
"The LORD is my portion and my inheritance," says my soul;
"therefore I have hope in Him and wait expectantly for Him."

LAMENTATIONS 3:22–24 AMP

When everything all around and within you seems to be coming
apart—including your dreams, plans, and hopes—it's hard to focus
on anything else. You may lament, "'Everything I had hoped for from
the LORD is lost!' The thought of my suffering and homelessness is
bitter beyond words. I will never forget this awful time, as I grieve
over my loss" (Lamentations 3:18–20 NLT).

Yet amid all your hardships, you must "still dare to hope" (Lamentations 3:21 NLT). You must remember that God's love is faithful.
It will never end. And it's because of that love that you will not stay
down and out.

Today and every day, remind yourself that God's faithfulness is
beyond measure. His mercies come fresh to you every morning. He's
yours. So live and breathe in hope!

Thank You, Lord, for Your continual love, Your abundant mercies
that greet me anew each morning. Because You are in my life, I will
continue to hope and pray—to expect Your good to come my way!

PRAYER JAR INSPIRATION:

Because God remains faithful to me, I will dare to hope!

HOPE THROUGH PRAYERS

*At the same time also prepare a guest room for me [in expectation
of a visit], for I hope that through your prayers I will be [granted
the gracious privilege of] coming to you [at Colossae].*

PHILEMON 22 AMP

Nothing in your life seems to be going the way you thought it would.
Your expectations of things getting better are falling by the wayside.
And then a fellow sister in Christ tells you she's been praying for you;
she's been asking God to bring an abundance of good your way, to
more than fulfill your many needs, small and great.

When you hear her words, you cannot help but feel her and God's
precious love. Your hope is revived. Because of the abundance of good
she began rolling your way through her prayers, you cannot help but
feel joy, knowing it was God who prompted her to fold her hands in
prayer for you.

Prayer reaches over houses, communities, states, and time zones,
bringing much-needed good to those who are praying and those
who are prayed for. Today, pray that God would bring an abundance
of good and hope into the lives of others. And all will be rewarded!

Lord, who would You prompt me to pray for today?

PRAYER JAR INSPIRATION:

When prayer is in my hands, the hope of good will be restored in others.

GOOD IN ABUNDANCE

He took the five loaves and the two fish, and looking up to heaven, He blessed and broke them. He kept giving them to the disciples to set before the crowd. Everyone ate and was filled. Then they picked up 12 baskets of leftover pieces.

LUKE 9:16–17 HCSB

Jesus had gone into the wilderness, and a crowd had followed Him. So He talked to them about God and His kingdom. He healed those who were sick. As evening approached, the disciples asked Jesus to send the people away. They had nothing to feed such a huge crowd—only five loaves of bread and two fish. That certainly wasn't enough to feed five thousand men along with all the women and children with them.

But Jesus told the disciples to have the people sit down. He then blessed the meager meal, broke it up, and kept giving the pieces to the disciples to distribute to the crowd. In the end, everyone had eaten their fill—and there were twelve baskets filled with leftovers!

Give what you have to God. He will not only bless it but increase it beyond what you could ever hope or imagine. For He cannot help but satisfy your hungry soul with an abundance of good.

I offer to You what I have, Lord. Bless it and me!

PRAYER JAR INSPIRATION:

God increases my offerings more than I could ever hope or imagine!

REALIZING GOD'S GOOD

Jacob awoke from his sleep and he said, "Without any doubt the Lord is in this place, and I did not realize it."

Genesis 28:16 AMP

Sometimes we get so caught up in our own lives—work, family, church, friends, hobbies, and community, as well as our unique problems and issues—that we forget to look around us. We forget to add God to the equation or to open our eyes to what He might be doing in or near us.

Jacob tricked his older brother out of his blessing and his inheritance. Then, literally running for his life, Jacob headed to his uncle's home to find a wife. On the way, he stopped and lay down to sleep, using a stone for a pillow.

That night Jacob dreamed of a stairway to heaven that had angels climbing up and down between heaven and earth. God told Jacob He'd always be with him, that He'd watch over and provide for him wherever he went. When Jacob woke, he realized what he hadn't before—that God was in that place.

Today, open your eyes. Look for God, His work, His face. Listen for His voice. He is where you are, waiting to bless and keep you, to do you good.

God, open my eyes to Your good.

PRAYER JAR INSPIRATION:

May I walk in a hope-filled way, continually open to God's blessings.

SOMETHING NEW

This is what the LORD says—who makes a way in the sea, and
a path through surging waters. . ."Do not remember the past
events, pay no attention to things of old. Look, I am about to
do something new; even now it is coming. Do you not see it?
Indeed, I will make a way in the wilderness, rivers in the desert."
ISAIAH 43:16, 18–19 HCSB

We are creatures of habit. Being so makes it easy for us to get stuck in a rut. We find it hard to imagine, to see, or to expect something new coming our way. Besides, there's comfort to be found in what's normal.

Yet God is always thinking up something new—something outside the box, unexpected, and wonderful. Remember, He's the One who made a path in the Red Sea so the Israelites could escape the thundering horses pulling the bloodthirsty Egyptians in their grand chariots.

Today, get your mind away from the old, the ordinary, the routine. Forget about what has gone before. Look for the new and good thing God is bringing your way. See how He is going to make a new path for you in the wilderness!

My eyes are off the old and looking for new good in You, Lord!

PRAYER JAR INSPIRATION:

Help me, Lord, to hope in something new from You!

CLINGING TO
HOPE AND FAITH

*Throwing off his cloak, he sprang up and came to Jesus. And
Jesus said to him, "What do you want me to do for you?" And the
blind man said to him, "Rabbi, let me recover my sight." And Jesus
said to him, "Go your way; your faith has made you well."*

MARK 10:50–52 ESV

As Jesus, His disciples, and the crowd following them made their way
out of Jericho, they passed Bartimaeus, a blind beggar who happened
to be sitting on the side of the road. When he heard it was Jesus
walking by him, he cried out for His mercy. And when people told
him to be quiet, Bartimaeus cried out even more!

So Jesus had them call the blind man to Him. In his eagerness
to get to Jesus, Bartimaeus threw off his coat and ran to Him. Jesus
asked him what he wanted. Bartimaeus said, "Rabbi, I want to see."

Jesus replied, "Go; your faith [and confident trust in My power]
has made you well" (Mark 10:52 AMP).

Consider what you may need to shrug off so that you can receive
the good that God wants to give you. Cling to the hope and faith
that Jesus can and will give you exactly what you need.

Lord, I cling to my hope and faith in Your goodness.

PRAYER JAR INSPIRATION:

Today I will shrug off _____ to receive _____ from Jesus.

GOOD INTENTS

*A woman who had suffered from a hemorrhage for twelve
years came up behind Him and touched the [tassel] fringe
of His outer robe; for she had been saying to herself,
"If I only touch His outer robe, I will be healed."*

MATTHEW 9:20–21 AMP

Self-talk can be a good thing. That is, *if* what you're telling yourself is
aligned with God's promises, who Jesus is, and what truth the Spirit
would have you understand. Such was the case with the woman who
had an issue of blood.

This poor woman had been hemorrhaging for twelve years. She'd
seen many doctors who took her money but left her no better off. So
when she heard that Jesus was coming her way, she made an effort
to reach out to Him, telling herself, "If I only touch His outer robe,
I will be healed."

Because of the good she hoped for, expected, prayed for, believed
in, and acted on, Jesus' power went out from Him to heal her. Seeing
her, He said, "Take courage, daughter; your [personal trust and con-
fident] faith [in Me] has made you well" (Matthew 9:22 AMP). And
in that moment, she was made whole.

*Help me, Lord, to hope for, expect, pray for, believe in,
and act on the fact that You intend good for me. Amen.*

PRAYER JAR INSPIRATION:

May my faith in God's good intentions make me hopeful and whole.

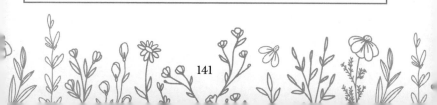

SEEKING GOOD

The desire of the righteous brings only good, but the expectation of the wicked brings wrath. . . . He who diligently seeks good seeks favor and grace, but he who seeks evil, evil will come to him.

PROVERBS 11:23, 27 AMP

Everyone has desires, hopes, and expectations. And what they hope for—whether consciously or unconsciously—they get. Consider Mordecai (the good guy) and Haman (the bad man) from the story of Esther.

The king's highest official, Haman, was angered that Mordecai the Jew would not bow to him. Plotting for Mordecai's death, Haman talked King Xerxes of Persia into signing an order that all Jews in the empire be destroyed.

When Mordecai got word of the plot, he went to Esther, his adopted daughter who was now the queen, and asked for her help, hoping she could thwart the evil plot and save her people by speaking to the king.

In the end, Haman was killed on the gallows meant for Mordecai. The king gave Haman's house and riches to Esther and Haman's prior position to Mordecai.

When a person's desires, hopes, and expectations are aligned with good, they will be rewarded with favor and grace. For God loves to answer the prayers of those right with Him.

Lord God, help me seek and expect only good.

PRAYER JAR INSPIRATION:

I pray my hopes and desires will bring only good to myself and others.

GOOD GIFTS

"You parents—if your children ask for a loaf of bread, do you give them a stone instead? Or if they ask for a fish, do you give them a snake? Of course not! So if you sinful people know how to give good gifts to your children, how much more will your heavenly Father give good gifts to those who ask him."

MATTHEW 7:9–11 NLT

Jesus tells us that God will give us what we ask for, what we seek. He will open the doors we come knocking on. Like any good parent, God will not give us a stone if we ask for bread. He won't give us a snake if we ask for a fish. If we, who have made mistakes, give good things to our children, how much more will our perfect God give good gifts to us!

Knowing this, we must make sure we go into our prayer closets with a strong expectation of receiving something good from God. We must look at Him as our compassionate and loving Father who wants to do all He can to give us joy, to equip us to serve Him.

I come to You in prayer today, Father, hoping— expecting—to receive nothing but good from You!

PRAYER JAR INSPIRATION:

Because I know my Father God is a giver of good gifts, my hope may be restored, my prayers more powerful!

PRAY AND PRAISE REGARDLESS!

Paul and Silas were praying and singing hymns of praise to God, and the prisoners were listening to them; suddenly there was a great earthquake, so [powerful] that the very foundations of the prison were shaken and at once all the doors were opened and everyone's chains were unfastened.

ACTS 16:25–26 AMP

While Paul and Silas were on their way to pray, they met a slave girl whose fortune-telling talents had made a great amount of money for her masters. After Paul exorcised her of this spirit, her owners dragged Paul and Silas to the magistrates in the marketplace and made charges against them. Then a mob stripped the duo of their clothes and beat them with rods, and the men were thrown into prison with their feet clamped in stocks.

Even though all these hardships had come upon them, Paul and Silas prayed and sang praises to God. In return, God sent an earthquake to shake up the jail, open its doors, and unfasten all the prisoners' chains.

This story teaches us that when we pray and sing praises to God regardless of our circumstances, He will bring us a wealth of good—and then some!

I am a woman of Your Way, Lord, ready to pray and praise every day!

PRAYER JAR INSPIRATION:

No matter what my circumstances, my hope for God's good reigns!

EYES UP

Therefore if you have been raised with Christ [to a new life, sharing in His resurrection from the dead], keep seeking the things that are above, where Christ is, seated at the right hand of God. Set your mind and keep focused habitually on the things above [the heavenly things], not on things that are on the earth [which have only temporal value].

COLOSSIANS 3:1–2 AMP

You've had a pretty good week. The next morning you awaken with great expectations for the day ahead. That's when the dishwasher breaks—and its warranty expired last week. Or one of the kids missed the bus. In your rush to drive your child to school before you head to work, you accidentally spill coffee on the report you spent weeks on. Or you head down to the basement to let the puppy out of its playpen, only to discover it had gotten itself out the night before and began eating your drywall.

All the things that can and sometimes do go wrong in one day are enough to drive a woman to the brink of tears. But God doesn't want you to go down that road. He'd rather you lift your eyes off these earthly things and focus on heavenly ones. The good things. The things that really matter. When you do, He'll give you the strength to deal with the rest.

Help me keep my eyes on Your heavenly good, Lord.

PRAYER JAR INSPIRATION:

Today my eyes are on You, Lord! Things are looking up!

NO LACK OF GOOD

*Oh, taste and see that the L*ORD *is good! Blessed is the man who takes refuge in him! Oh, fear the L*ORD*, you his saints, for those who fear him have no lack! The young lions suffer want and hunger; but those who seek the L*ORD *lack no good thing.*

PSALM 34:8–10 ESV

Those who obey God, who revere Him as their Lord and Savior, Creator and Sustainer, will find there is no one better than He. For no one and nothing in the world is *greater* than He.

So, at the first sign of trouble, don't count on yourself to work your way through it. Instead, run to the Lord. Take refuge in His protection, soak up the peace of His presence, breathe in His wisdom. Know that when you are hidden in Him, nothing can harm you.

When you walk with God—minding His Way, asking His advice, *and then taking it!*—you will surely lack nothing. After all, He is your all in all—your comfort, your calm, your faithful Friend who is always looking to bless you with all good things.

Thank You, Lord, for always being there for me, providing refuge, making sure I lack no good thing—including hope in You. It is You alone I love with all my heart, soul, and mind.

PRAYER JAR INSPIRATION:

In and with God, I lack absolutely nothing.

146

HOPE
for Security

Most everyone wants to feel a sense of security. Some people hope for and try to find it in marriage, a good job, bank accounts, insurance policies, or property. But the truth is our security in things of this earth is uncertain. These things are false security, and they won't give the kind of inner peace and lasting security we seek.

Our security is in the Lord, not in people or things. If we put our faith and trust in our heavenly Father, even in unpleasant times, we have the assurance that bad things cannot devour us. We are secure in His hands. "In the fear of the LORD is strong confidence: and his children shall have a place of refuge" (Proverbs 14:26 KJV).

Maybe you're going through a difficult or seemingly impossible situation today, and you feel completely hopeless. In our darkest hour, God is always there, waiting to help. We only need to call out to Him in prayer. When we feel that there is no hope, God does His greatest work so that His name is glorified. Whatever situation you may be faced with today, you can trust the Lord. You are secure in His hands.

OUR ANCHOR

*By two unchangeable things [His promise and His oath] in
which it is impossible for God to lie, we who have fled [to Him]
for refuge would have strong encouragement and indwelling
strength to hold tightly to the hope set before us. This hope
[this confident assurance] we have as an anchor of the soul.*

HEBREWS 6:18–19 AMP

God told Abraham that He would bless and multiply him. And Abraham, having waited patiently for God to make good on that promise, obtained it (Hebrews 6:13–15).

We are heirs of that promise and all the others God makes through His Word. And we know He'll make good on them because God never goes back on His word. All we need do is continue following in His Way, believe His promises, and patiently await their fulfillment, assured that Jesus has created an unbreakable spiritual lifeline between us and our Maker.

F. B. Meyer wrote, "Your prayers cannot be lost, as ships at sea; they will make harbor at last, laden with golden freight. . . . Hope is *sure*, because the anchor has fastened in a sure ground; *steadfast*, because its cable will not snap in the strain; and *entering, etc.*, because it unites us to the unseen. Jesus has taken our anchor into the inner harbor, and has dropped it down into the clear, still water there."*

Thank You, Lord, for the steadfast hope I have in You.

PRAYER JAR INSPIRATION:

With Jesus, I am anchored on hope.

---

* https://www.studylight.org/commentaries/eng/fbm/hebrews-6.html

PICK A TREE

"Blessed [with spiritual security] is the man who
believes and trusts in and relies on the LORD and
whose hope and confident expectation is the LORD."

JEREMIAH 17:7 AMP

Speaking through Jeremiah, God tells us the difference between the life of the woman who trusts in her fellow humans and she who trusts in Him. In the first scenario, the woman who makes her fellow creatures her strength and turns her heart from God is cursed. She will be like a stunted shrub in the desert, "with no hope for the future," living in a "barren wilderness, in an uninhabited salty land" (Jeremiah 17:6 NLT).

On the other side of the tree line is the woman who makes God her hope and confidence. She will be blessed with spiritual security. She will be like a tree "planted along a riverbank, with roots that reach deep into the water. Such trees are not bothered by the heat or worried by long months of drought. Their leaves stay green, and they never stop producing fruit" (Jeremiah 17:8 NLT).

What kind of woman, what kind of tree, would you like to be?

Lord, help me to believe in You, to rely on You above
all other people and things. Help me become a woman
who is confidently trusting and hoping in You!

PRAYER JAR INSPIRATION:

Bless me, my Lord, as I turn to and hope in You for everything.

MOST HIGH SHELTER

*He who dwells in the shelter of the Most High will remain secure
and rest in the shadow of the Almighty [whose power no enemy can
withstand]. I will say of the LORD, "He is my refuge and my fortress, my
God, in whom I trust [with great confidence, and on whom I rely]!"*

PSALM 91:1–2 AMP

When you need to find a safe space, your best bet is in God. In Him,
you can find the rest you need for He is the Almighty! No enemy
can withstand His power!

Are you frightened? Stressed? Unprotected? Vulnerable? Then run
to God. He'll save you from the fowler's snares. Like a mother eagle,
He'll cover you with His wings. If any trouble does come your way,
you'll be a spectator to it only. When you make God your refuge, no evil
can befall you; He will command His angels to guard and defend you.

How can you get there from here? By loving God. By knowing
who He is. By trusting in Him, knowing He will never abandon you.
When you do these things, you can call on God, and He will answer
you. He will be with you in trouble, He will rescue and honor you.
He will cover you with His presence.

*You, Lord, are my Refuge and Fortress,
the God in whom I trust and hide!*

PRAYER JAR INSPIRATION:

My hope and heart reside in the refuge of the Most High.

EXPECTATIONS

The lame man looked at them eagerly, expecting some money.
But Peter said, "I don't have any silver or gold for you. But I'll give you
what I have. In the name of Jesus Christ the Nazarene, get up and walk!"

ACTS 3:5–6 NLT

Apostles Peter and John were heading to the temple for prayer. As they approached, they saw a man lying beside the Beautiful Gate. Lame since birth, he was carried to that gate every day so that he could beg for money from temple-goers.

When the man saw Peter and John approaching, he looked at them with hope in his eyes, expecting them to give him some money. But Peter said that instead of money he would give what he had—healing in Jesus' name. Peter then grabbed the man's arm and raised him up. All at once the man's feet and ankles were filled with strength, allowing the man to leap, stand, and walk, praising God.

Your best security, help, and answer to prayer lie in looking to God, not to money. Today, take your problem, your expectations, your hopes and dreams to Jesus Christ, knowing that in His power, you will receive exactly what you need.

I look to You, Lord, for all that I need.

PRAYER JAR INSPIRATION:

My eager expectations lie in Jesus.

RELIANCE

*We were crushed and overwhelmed beyond our ability to endure,
and we thought we would never live through it. In fact, we
expected to die. But as a result, we stopped relying on ourselves
and learned to rely only on God, who raises the dead.*

2 Corinthians 1:8–9 nlt

This world can be a very difficult place. There may be days when you feel crushed and overwhelmed. You may begin to think that you can endure no more of the political unrest, wars, disease, violence, abuse, famine, and natural disasters that plague earth's inhabitants. You may begin to believe you'll never make it through to the dawn of the next day.

To rise above that depressed state, you must stop relying on yourself and learn to rely on God. As soon as you do, a calm will begin to sweep over you. When you give yourself into God's hands, you will find yourself in the most secure and loving place you can ever imagine on this side of heaven.

When you are crushed by trouble, look to God for all. Be secure in the knowledge that He who can raise the dead can and will save you.

> *Help me, Lord, even before the day of trouble
> comes, to rely on You instead of myself.*

PRAYER JAR INSPIRATION:

My hope of rescue lies in the God who can raise the dead.

WELL-PLACED CONFIDENCE

*And he did rescue us from mortal danger, and he will rescue
us again. We have placed our confidence in him, and he will
continue to rescue us. And you are helping us by praying for us.*

2 Corinthians 1:10–11 nlt

When you had no hope of surviving a mortal danger, when all you
saw was certain death on your horizon, you learned to rely on God
instead of yourself. And He saved you. Now, knowing God can do it
once, you're certain He'll do so again. At least for a little while.

We humans have short memories. When life calms down a bit,
we may once more begin relying on ourselves instead of God. After
all, we can handle anything, really. . . . Can't we?

No. We can't. Every breath is a gift from God, and so we must continually work to put and keep our confidence in Him, our Good Shepherd,
knowing He is our constant rescuer even from hazards we may never see!

Prayers from others will help us continue to rely on God alone. So
today, choose someone that you would willingly pray for daily. And
ask that person to pray for you. In doing so, you'll be helping each
other remember to be securely confident in God.

*Who, Lord, would You have me pray for in my
effort to help them keep their confidence in You?*

PRAYER JAR INSPIRATION:

My continual hope and confidence rest in God and prayer!

SOUL SHELTER

Be gracious to me, O God, be gracious and merciful to me, for my soul finds shelter and safety in You, and in the shadow of Your wings I will take refuge and be confidently secure until destruction passes by.

PSALM 57:1 AMP

King Saul was relentlessly hunting down David. When the latter and his men took refuge in a cave, it turned out to be the exact same cave that Saul later went in to relieve himself. David was so close to the king, he could have touched him!

When we're in the thick of trouble, the safest and most secure place to be is in God. There alone will our souls find the shelter they need to stay calm and escape harm until the calamity passes by.

David rested in the assurance that everything God had promised him would come to pass, for He was as good as His word. David had no doubts about God, singing, "He will send from heaven and save me" (Psalm 57:3 AMP).

When you're in dire straits and you need a secure refuge, a shelter for your soul, fly to God. Rest yourself in Him, confident He is that safest place you can be. Allow His peace to permeate your entire being. And when the danger has passed by, be sure to praise Him.

God Most High, be the shelter and refuge
for my soul when danger comes to call.

PRAYER JAR INSPIRATION:

God is my forever place of safety.

DEATH-DEFYING REFUGE

The wicked is overthrown through his wrongdoing, but the righteous
has hope and confidence and a refuge [with God] even in death.

PROVERBS 14:32 AMP

Cruel and wicked people (think Jezebel) are driven away from God's favor and His presence. They do not keep company with those who are right with God. They will forever remain separate from any hope of happiness—in this life and the next. After death, they may try to run to God for help but will soon find themselves driven away from the door.

Things are, of course, different for those who are in good standing with God. She who is righteous (think Hannah) can fly to God amid the calamities and catastrophes in life. She can pour her heart out to Him in prayer, talk to Him when her heart is crushed. She knows she will find a safe place in, receive comfort from, and garner a listening ear with God because all her confidence is in Him. Even when she faces death, she has hope that she will be delivered to a life everlasting.

Today, remember where your hope and confidence lie: in the everlasting, death-defying refuge of God.

To You, Lord, I fly for safety, knowing You are
and will be my sure Refuge, even in death.

PRAYER JAR INSPIRATION:

My hope and safety lie in God, my refuge in life and death.

TAKE HEART

"An angel of the God I belong to and serve stood by me, and said,
'Don't be afraid, Paul. You must stand before Caesar. And, look!
God has graciously given you all those who are sailing with you.'"

Acts 27:22–24 HCSB

The apostle Paul had been put aboard a ship sailing for Rome so that he could stand before Caesar. As time went by, the voyage became more and more dangerous.

Finally, the sailors thought they were on the right tack. Then a storm came upon them. The men sailing with Paul began to think their situation was hopeless. But Paul urged them to take heart. An angel had told him they would survive. And Paul had great faith "in God that it will be exactly as I have been told" (Acts 27:25 ESV).

God has a plan for your life, just as He did for Paul's. And nothing in heaven or on earth can change or disrupt that plan. So take heart. Don't be afraid. Have faith in God that it will be exactly as you have been told.

I fear nothing, Lord, knowing that because of Your presence
and promises, all will be well in this life and the next.

PRAYER JAR INSPIRATION:

The presence of God and His angels
among us buoys my hope and faith.

156

WALL OF FIRE

" 'For I,' declares the Lord, 'will be a wall of fire around her
[protecting her from enemies], and I will be the glory in her midst.' "
. . . "Sing for joy and rejoice, O Daughter of Zion; for behold, I
am coming, and I will dwell in your midst," declares the Lord.

ZECHARIAH 2:5, 10 AMP

You are a woman of the Way. As such, you have a unique role to play in God's grand plan. For only a woman of your strength, history, and makeup can do what He needs to be specifically done. And because you are precious to Him, He will find a way to protect you while you are playing your part.

So, when you find yourself feeling insecure, defenseless, and vulnerable, remember that you are the daughter of an eternal King. He is your Shield, your Help—the wall of fire that surrounds you, protecting you from anything and anyone that might dare to cause you harm.

Woman of the Way, God dwells in your midst. So do not quiver in fear, but stand strong, fast, and firm. You do not walk alone but with the almighty God, whose power no foe can withstand.

Thank You, Lord, for being not only my life coach
and planner but my great Protector. With You in
my midst, I can and will walk with confidence.

PRAYER JAR INSPIRATION:

God is my fire wall.

WINGS OF REFUGE

"Everything you have done for your mother-in-law. . .has been fully reported to me: how you left your father and mother and the land of your birth, and how you came to a people you didn't previously know. May the LORD reward you for what you have done, and may you receive a full reward from the LORD God of Israel, under whose wings you have come for refuge."

RUTH 2:11–12 HCSB

All those kindnesses you have done for others and all the ways you have stepped out of your comfort zone are things people—believers and nonbelievers alike—take notice of. It is that kind of kindness and courage that makes people want what you have.

Your life may sometimes seem like an obstacle course as you meet challenge after challenge in your attempt to do the right thing: to help others selflessly. To walk with them when the road gets tough. But the end goal is finding your unique and secure place in the refuge of God.

Today, may the Lord reward you for what you have done and will do as you seek your place of refuge in Him.

Help me, Lord, to meet the challenges
of this life as I steer my course to You.

PRAYER JAR INSPIRATION:

Under God's wings I find my eternal reward and refuge.

LIVING IMAGE

He is the exact living image [the essential manifestation] of the unseen
God [the visible representation of the invisible], the firstborn [the
preeminent one, the sovereign, and the originator] of all creation. . . .
And He Himself existed and is before all things, and in Him all things
hold together. [His is the controlling, cohesive force of the universe.]

Colossians 1:15, 17 amp

When everything feels like it's falling apart, God's followers need not become uneasy or discouraged. Because Jesus is with us. He's holding everything together—from our frail bodies to the entire universe.

And Jesus has not left us without the knowledge of who God is. All we must do is look at the Son, the living image of the holy Father. When we read about Jesus in the Word, we perceive that He is love personified. That He has not left us alone, but His Spirit remains with us. That He longs for us to be His companion, follower, and replica, a sensitive soul with empathy for the lost, hurt, broken, and afraid.

In the knowledge of all these things—in the fact that Jesus, love personified, is continually and constantly with us, showing us how to live as He lived—we find our hope, security, and peace.

Firstborn of my Father God, work and dwell
within me. Hold me together. Be my living hope.

PRAYER JAR INSPIRATION:

Jesus, thank You for the hope I find in Your
presence within and without.

NEVER-ENDING STORY

*Let us who live in the light be clearheaded, protected by the armor
of faith and love, and wearing as our helmet the confidence
of our salvation. For God chose to save us through our Lord
Jesus Christ. . . . Christ died for us so that, whether we are dead
or alive when he returns, we can live with him forever.*

1 Thessalonians 5:8–10 NLT

Because we believe in Jesus, because we accepted Him as our Savior,
we are children of the light (1 Thessalonians 5:5). As such, we do not
live unprotected. We have surrounding us an impenetrable armor
of faith and love. On our heads we wear a helmet of the hope of
salvation. No matter where we are, regardless of whether we are alive
or dead when Jesus returns, we can have the confidence that we will
live with Him forever.

Yes, life on earth can be difficult at times. We will have our fair
share of heartaches. But through good times and bad, we can live and
die secure in the knowledge that our story with Jesus will never end.

*Thank You, Jesus, for making me a child of Your light. For
protecting me with Your love. For being my happily ever after.*

PRAYER JAR INSPIRATION:

With Jesus in my life, I live a never-ending story.

CONFIDENCE
AND COURAGE

O God, my heart is steadfast [with confident faith]; I will sing, I will sing praises, even with my soul. . . . For Your lovingkindness is great and higher than the heavens; Your truth reaches to the skies. . . . Deliverance by man is in vain [a worthless hope]. With God we will do valiantly.

PSALM 108:1, 4, 12–13 AMP

God has more love for you than you could ever imagine. And because of His love, you can live without worry or fear. Your heart can be warmed by your ever-present trust and firm faith in Him. No matter what's happening, no matter how many things skitter out of your control, no matter how many people desert you, no matter what comes against you. . .you have God, the supreme and holy Being, in your corner—not just rooting for you, guiding you, and protecting you but fighting for you.

With God in your life, with Him walking by your side, you have all you need to be a confident and courageous woman, one who will live and do fearlessly.

I sing praises to You today, Lord. For with You, I have the courage and confidence to be what You would have me be and to do what You would have me do.

PRAYER JAR INSPIRATION:

God is my worthy hope, the Author and Supplier of my confidence and courage.

INDEPENDENTLY GODLY

Teach those who are rich in this world not to be proud and not to trust in their money, which is so unreliable. Their trust should be in God, who richly gives us all we need for our enjoyment. Tell them to use their money to do good. They should be rich in good works and generous to those in need, always being ready to share with others.

1 TIMOTHY 6:17–18 NLT

Some women think they can only really live, can only really enjoy their lives, if they have enough money in the bank to allow them to spend as they please. They believe they will only be truly happy if they can keep up with the Joneses, take a nice vacation, have the bigger house, or buy that darling outfit they saw advertised online.

If thoughts like these start wending their way through your head, you can be sure danger lies ahead.

Money is an uncertain commodity. If you trust in that today, you will fall tomorrow. Instead of trusting in money, bank on the only thing that is certain: God. He'll supply all you need—and leave you enough left over to share with others.

Strive to be godly, not wealthy.

In You I trust, Lord. Not in the almighty dollar. Show me today who You would have me spend Your love on.

PRAYER JAR INSPIRATION:

I trust and hope in the God of plenty.

THE FLOURISHING WOMAN

The godly will flourish like palm trees and grow strong like the cedars of Lebanon. For they are transplanted to the Lord's own house. They flourish in the courts of our God. Even in old age they will still produce fruit; they will remain vital and green.

PSALM 92:12–14 NLT

Our bodies are finite structures. As the years go by, our earth suits will eventually give out on us. Yet even then, if we stay close to the Lord, if we continue to obey, love, follow, and worship Him, we will remain a vital part of His body. We will be like the strong cedars of Lebanon, still green and able to produce fruit.

Today, make sure you are nourishing yourself in the Lord. Spend time in His Word, seeing it not as a chore but as opening a window to wisdom that will help you through your day. Stay steady in prayer, and afterward spend some time in God's presence. In doing so, you will not only be nourished but also find yourself flourishing in God's house for all your days.

I want to grow closer to You and in You, Lord, so that I can continue to be a viable and vital part of Your kingdom today and every day of my life.

PRAYER JAR INSPIRATION:

In God, I find my hope nourished and my heart flourishing.

WAIT AND HOPE

Are there any among the idols of the nations who can send rain? Or can the heavens [of their own will] give showers? Is it not You, O Lᴏʀᴅ our God? Therefore we will wait and hope [confidently] in You, for You are the one who has made all these things [the heavens and the rain].

Jᴇʀᴇᴍɪᴀʜ 14:22 AMP

In this world, many worship the false gods of power, wealth, and fame. People seem willing to do anything to rise above others, to accumulate money, to obtain their fifteen minutes of fame. But none of those things, none of those "gods," can send rain. None can make the heavens pour down the water that we and our planet need. No one but God can save the bees, bats, and birds, the oceans, rivers, and lakes.

When you need something—when you are living in famine or drought, flood or fire—apply to God and Him alone. Acknowledge Him as Lord over all things seen and unseen. Then wait and hope with confidence in Him, that He who made the sky, clouds, earth, wind, and water will come through for you.

You, Lord, are my only God, my only security on this orb of earth. To You alone I pray. Upon You alone I wait. In You alone I hope.

PRAYER JAR INSPIRATION:

You only, Lord, are my God and hope.

THE SATISFIER

The Lord always keeps his promises; he is gracious in all he does. The Lord helps the fallen and lifts those bent beneath their loads. The eyes of all look to you in hope; you give them their food as they need it. When you open your hand, you satisfy the hunger and thirst of every living thing.

<small>PSALM 145:13–16 NLT</small>

God is not like people. He never breaks a promise. He is not out for Himself alone. He is not blind to the burdens of others. That's why you can trust Him and live your life for Him.

When you are afraid or under pressure, look to God's promises. Find one that fits your situation, and sink your spirit into it. When it seems no one has any mercy or compassion for others, turn to the Bible stories where Jesus loves, heals, or lifts another; imagine yourself as the one He has helped. When you have fallen or can no longer get out from under that burden you've been bearing, ask God to help you up, to take on your load.

See God as the open hand that holds all you will ever hunger or thirst for on both sides of heaven. Tell Him what you need, and He will ensure you are satisfied and secure.

You, Lord, hold all I need, want, and wish for.
Thank You for looking after me in all ways, always.

PRAYER JAR INSPIRATION:

My eyes look to God in hope and love.

FAITHFUL LOVE

"Oh, Lord God! You Yourself made the heavens and earth by Your great power and with Your outstretched arm. Nothing is too difficult for You! You show faithful love to thousands. . .great and mighty God whose name is Yahweh of Hosts, the One great in counsel and mighty in deed."

JEREMIAH 32:17–19 HCSB

Do you know who God really is? He's the One who, by His great power and outstretched arm, made the heavens and the earth. He formed the very heavens that lie above your head, that reach into galaxies and universes humankind has yet to uncover and discover! He created the very planet you are sitting, lying, standing on! He designed by hand the earth that rotates, the sun that shines on it, the moon that revolves around it. God made this orb that feeds and waters you, the one on which you first began your earthly life and will hold your body when you pass on to the other side.

This God for whom nothing is impossible loves you. When you feel insecure, remember who holds you every night and leads you every day. Then rest easy, knowing God's got you. With Him, anything is possible.

God of all creation and power, by You I stand and rest.
Hold me close day and night. In Jesus' name and love. Amen.

PRAYER JAR INSPIRATION:

God's faithful love and immense power rock
me to sleep and awaken me to a new dawn.

YOUR SHELTER

I will sing praises to your name, O Most High. My enemies
retreated; they staggered and died when you appeared. . . .
The Lord is a shelter for the oppressed, a refuge in times
of trouble. Those who know your name trust in you.

PSALM 9:2–3, 9–10 NLT

God is amazing—and He is on your side!

When you're in trouble, when enemies seem to have surrounded you, just call on God. Ask for His help. Remember what has happened in times past when God has come on the scene—the calm He brings amid calamity, the strength He bears against every foe.

God can not only make forces that seem impenetrable stagger and fall but also repel them so that they begin to retreat, never to show their faces again! Meanwhile, for you He creates a place of safety. He shelters you; He hides you behind His hand until trouble passes by. When the dust has settled, when the spoils left behind by your enemies are ready to be plucked, only then will He open the shelter, allowing you to see what remains for you to glean.

Today, sing praises to your Refuge, Shelter, and Provider.

You, Lord, are my amazing all in all!
Thank You for sheltering me in every storm.

PRAYER JAR INSPIRATION:

God, my sure Shelter and everlasting song, it is You I praise!

HELP AND RESCUE

I prayed to the LORD, and he answered me. He freed me from all my fears. . . . The angel of the LORD is a guard; he surrounds and defends all who fear him. . . . The LORD hears his people when they call to him for help. He rescues them from all their troubles.

PSALM 34:4, 7, 17 NLT

Humans sometimes get the idea that they are self-sufficient—that they can handle anything that comes their way. Yet time and time again, they are proved wrong.

God wants you to know He is here for you. He is just waiting for you to call on Him, to acknowledge that you do indeed need Him. For when you allow Him into your life, He will free you from all the fears you have been harboring for so long.

God is the Guide who goes before you and the Guard who protects you from behind. He will surround you and defend you from whatever comes against you.

Today, consider all the things you have been trying to battle on your own. Then enter a time of prayer, asking God to take them all on His own massive shoulders. He will hear your calls for help and rescue you.

Lord, save me from those fears that tie me down. Rescue me from all that plagues me. I place myself completely in Your hands. Amen.

PRAYER JAR INSPIRATION:

God is my hope and help, my fear fighter!

HOPE
for Guidance

Have you ever been at a crossroads in your life and needed guidance? I'm sure we all have been at some point. Making decisions is a common dilemma. When it comes to our hope for guidance, we should never depend solely on ourselves. As Christians, we want to be sure that God is guiding us in the right direction. "Trust in the LORD with all thine heart; and lean not unto thine own understanding. In all thy ways acknowledge him, and he shall direct thy paths" (Proverbs 3:5–6 KJV).

God will guide us in our everyday living. We can call on Him to direct our path in each decision and development. All we need to do is acknowledge Him, trust Him, and depend on Him and not ourselves. The truth is we really can't make it without His help.

God has a special plan for every believer, and He wants us to trust Him with our whole heart. There are four principles for receiving God's guidance. (1) We must know His Word, which comes from reading the Bible. (2) We should be completely committed to doing God's will. (3) We have to trust that He will provide everything necessary to fulfill His will for our lives. (4) We need to pray, expecting God to grant us wisdom. We can live victoriously if we seek God's wisdom and guidance for our lives.

WALKING IN THE WAY

This is what the Lord says—your Redeemer, the Holy One of Israel:
"I am the Lord your God, who teaches you what is good for you and
leads you along the paths you should follow. Oh, that you had listened
to my commands! Then you would have had peace flowing like a
gentle river and righteousness rolling over you like waves in the sea."

ISAIAH 48:17–18 NLT

Are you a woman who is walking in the Way of the Lord, looking to
God for direction, following His teachings, obeying the Holy Spirit?
Or are you a frazzled female who has lost every bit of peace she once
knew and rarely opens her ears to God's voice?

If you want to know the right way to go, if you want your life to
be filled with peace like a river and to have righteousness roll over
you like a wave, look to God to lead you. Don't go off on your own
but stay on the path outlined in His Word. Then you will gain all He
has provided for you—and so much more!

I'm looking to You, Lord. Teach me what is good. Lead
me along the right paths. Open my ears to Your voice,
my heart to Your love. In Jesus' name, amen.

PRAYER JAR INSPIRATION:

The right way is God's Way.

GOD'S CHART

"This Book of the Law shall not depart from your mouth, but you shall read [and meditate on] it day and night, so that you may be careful to do [everything] in accordance with all that is written in it; for then you will make your way prosperous, and then you will be successful."

JOSHUA 1:8 AMP

Henry Ward Beecher, an American preacher, said, "The Bible is God's chart for you to steer by, to keep you from the bottom of the sea, and to show you where the harbor is, and how to reach it without running on rocks or bars." Are you charting your course by the Word? Or are you too busy looking to the opinions of others, navigating by societal mores or religious traditions?

God wants you to sink yourself into His Word: to read it and meditate on it day and night. To navigate your life by its precepts and lessons. For only then will you prosper and succeed in all you do—perhaps not as the world sees prosperity and success but as God sees it, which is infinitely more stupendous and life changing.

Help me, Lord, to make time in my schedule to consult and meditate on Your Word. For Your Word is what I base my life on.

PRAYER JAR INSPIRATION:

God's Word is my hope and stay.

THE SHEPHERD

The Lord God will come with might, and His arm will rule for
Him. Most certainly His reward is with Him, and His restitution
accompanies Him. He will protect His flock like a shepherd, He
will gather the lambs in His arm, He will carry them in His bosom;
He will gently and carefully lead those nursing their young.

ISAIAH 40:10–11 AMP

There may be some times in your life when you feel very vulnerable or weak. Weary from constant attack, you can barely raise up your hands in prayer. You no longer know what to do or where to go.

There is no need to worry, to panic, to sink further. Instead, you may rise up in the certainty that God can come in His strength and make all things right. That He will fend off your enemies within and without. That He will protect you like a shepherd protects his sheep and will gather the young, the unsteady and carry them close to His heart. That He will gently lead the vulnerable, those spending their energy taking care of the needy.

Little lamb of God, follow your Shepherd. He will lead you the right way.

My Lord the Shepherd, come in Your strength. Protect
me from all that has come against me. Gather me
in Your arms, and gently lead me home to You.

PRAYER JAR INSPIRATION:

Gentle Lord, renew me with Your presence.
Lead me down Your pathway.

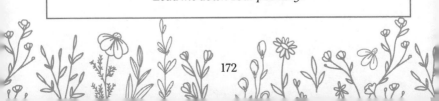

STILL LISTENING

Be still before the LORD; wait patiently for Him and entrust
yourself to Him; do not fret (whine, agonize) because of him who
prospers in his way, because of the man who carries out wicked
schemes. . . . Wait for and expect the LORD and keep His way.

PSALM 37:7, 34 AMP

When you pray, do you give God time to respond—or do you just pour out your heart and then walk away, not sitting still long enough to hear what He has to say? Or do you only pray for direction once, and then, in your desire to become as prosperous as the ungodly, determine your own strategy to obtain what you want, leaving God wordless, a silent figure standing on the sidelines?

If you don't allow God to speak after you've presented your requests to Him, you're not really praying. Author Madeleine L'Engle wrote, "To pray is to listen, to move through my own chattering to God, to that place where I can be silent and listen to what God may have to say."

Today, add listening to your prayer time. Determine to be still before the Lord, patiently waiting with open ears and heart, ready to hear what He may want to say.

Help me, Lord, to be a better listener, to be patient, to be still before You.

PRAYER JAR INSPIRATION:

In silence before God, I hope and wait.

A WOMAN'S WALK

*The steps of a [good and righteous] man are directed and
established by the Lord, and He delights in his way [and blesses
his path]. When he falls, he will not be hurled down, because
the Lord is the One who holds his hand and sustains him.*

PSALM 37:23–24 AMP

God is working out a plan for your life, one that fits into His grand
scheme. And because you are walking His Way, even when you
stumble, you won't be down for the count. God has a grip on your
hand, and He's never going to let go.

How wonderful that God, the Lord of the universe, the Creator and
master planner, has a plan. For you. Right now. In this moment. And
all you have to do to tune in to that plan—to listen to His voice—is
follow His Word, not letting the world bring you down or make you
deviate from your path.

Today, walk God's Way. Know that He'll keep you steady.

*Thank You, Lord, for showing me how and where to walk, for having
a firm grip on my hand, for making me a part of Your grand plan.*

PRAYER JAR INSPIRATION:

With God, I can and will find firm footing.

174

THE POWER OF GOD'S WORD

"The rain and snow come down from the heavens and stay on the ground to water the earth. They cause the grain to grow, producing seed for the farmer and bread for the hungry. It is the same with my word. I send it out, and it always produces fruit. It will accomplish all I want it to, and it will prosper everywhere I send it."

ISAIAH 55:10–11 NLT

God's Word has great power. Wherever He sends it, it accomplishes what He desires.

And you have access to that Word 24-7. Night and day, day and night, you can read His Word. Follow it. Pray it back to Him. Meditate on it. Study it. Love it. Rest on it. Hope in it. Be empowered and encouraged by it. Write it on your heart, and etch it into your mind.

No matter how many times you read the Bible, you can still find a new meaning to ponder, a new direction to take, a new vision to see. For God's Word is alive in power, in fruitfulness, in prosperity.

Today, open God's Word. Thank Him for giving you access to it. Then allow it, word by word, to direct your love and your life.

I open my heart, mind, soul, and spirit to Your Word today, Lord. May it take root within and produce heavenly fruit without.

PRAYER JAR INSPIRATION:

Oh, Word of God, grow deep within me.

LESSONS IN THE WORD

*Such things were written in the Scriptures long ago to teach us.
And the Scriptures give us hope and encouragement as we wait
patiently for God's promises to be fulfilled. May God, who gives this
patience and encouragement, help you live in complete harmony
with each other, as is fitting for followers of Christ Jesus.*

ROMANS 15:4–5 NLT

Sometimes life presents us with certain situations—times when we're not sure what to think, do, or say. We scour the Bible, looking for answers to specific questions or problems, wondering how we'll find help in a book that was put together almost two thousand years ago.

Although the stories in the Bible took place in ancient days and in places we may never have visited, the people in them were pretty much the same as the people you meet today. Humankind has not changed so drastically that we cannot imagine ourselves in the same scenarios as many of our Bible heroes and take heed of the lessons they learned.

For example, when you need to be brave, look to Esther, who was made queen for such a time as hers (Esther 4:14). When you're full of sorrow, look to Hannah, who poured her heart out to God (1 Samuel 1:15). And if you're not sure what pathway to take, take a cue from the things Jesus did, and do that (John 13:15).

Thank You, Lord, for the gift and guidance of Your Word.

PRAYER JAR INSPIRATION:

*Today I will scour God's lesson book,
my source of hope and encouragement.*

SHINING LIGHT

Jesus shouted to the crowds, "If you trust me, you are trusting not only me, but also God who sent me. For when you see me, you are seeing the one who sent me. I have come as a light to shine in this dark world, so that all who put their trust in me will no longer remain in the dark."

JOHN 12:44–46 NLT

No one enjoys stumbling around in the dark. It's too easy to stub our toes or trip over a piece of furniture and break something—including ourselves! Yet that's what happens when we stop opening up the Word and letting Jesus' light shine not just on us but on any situation we may find ourselves in.

Jesus told crowds of people that when they trusted in Him, they were also trusting in Father God. For He, Jesus, was the manifestation of God Himself! He also told them He was the light that had come to shine in this dark, dark world, and if they trusted in Him, they'd no longer be stumbling around in the dark.

Looking for a way in, up, or out? Open up the Word. Allow it to shine into your life and show you the way. Trust in that light, and you'll find yourself steady on your feet.

Lord, I trust in You and Your Word to show me the way through the darkness—to You.

PRAYER JAR INSPIRATION:

Jesus is the light of my life!

THOUGHTS AND WAYS

*Trust in the LORD with all your heart, and do not lean on
your own understanding. In all your ways acknowledge
him, and he will make straight your paths.*

PROVERBS 3:5–6 ESV

Many books written by experts remind us of how different the thoughts
and ways of women are from the thoughts and ways of men. It really
does seem as if the opposite sex is from Mars and we are from Venus!

Our thoughts and ways are different not just from men but from
God! And God reveals that very idea, telling us, "My thoughts are not
your thoughts, neither are your ways my ways. . . . For as the heavens
are higher than the earth, so are my ways higher than your ways and
my thoughts than your thoughts" (Isaiah 55:8–9 ESV).

Because our thoughts and ways are so alien next to God's, we must
trust Him with all our heart. We must lean on His wisdom, not ours.
We must seek His will in all things, knowing He—not we—will give
us the best guidance as to what path we should take.

*Although I don't understand many things, Lord, I trust You
to show me the right way to go, the right path to take.*

PRAYER JAR INSPIRATION:

*In God alone I trust, for He can show me
what to think, which way to go, how to hope.*

SLOWING DOWN

The LORD is my shepherd; there is nothing I lack. He lets me lie down in green pastures; He leads me beside quiet waters. He renews my life; He leads me along the right paths for His name's sake. Even when I go through the darkest valley, I fear no danger, for You are with me.

PSALM 23:1–4 HCSB

It is so easy to get frazzled these days. Everyone—you, the kids, the husband, the coworker, your boss, friends, other family members, even fellow churchgoers—seems to be in a hurry to get somewhere. Everyone's schedule seems to be full, *so* full that a woman can't help but feel like the proverbial chicken running around with her head chopped off! When we have lost sight of calm and are adrift in chaos, we need to slow down and bring to mind the familiar words of Psalm 23.

God is your Shepherd. With Him, you lack nothing. He'll get you to lie down in some soft green fields. He'll lead you beside those still waters where your soul and spirit can find refreshment and silence. He'll lead you where you are to go—on *His* schedule.

Even when things look dark, you don't need to fear anything. The Creator and Sustainer of the universe walks with you. Today, slow down and go with God.

In You, Good Shepherd, I find the peace and rest I crave.

PRAYER JAR INSPIRATION:

My Shepherd will lead me home to Him and His peace.

NO DEADLINES

"The vision is yet for the appointed [future] time. It hurries toward the goal [of fulfillment]; it will not fail. Even though it delays, wait [patiently] for it, because it will certainly come; it will not delay."

HABAKKUK 2:3 AMP

God has planted a dream within your heart. He's making your vision, your part of His plan, a reality. That's His job.

Your job is to wait for your dream's fulfillment—to not become impatient but to trust God to bring things to fruition. About this, preacher and author A. W. Tozer wrote, "God never hurries. There are no deadlines against which He must work. Only to know this is to quiet our spirits and relax our nerves."

So stay on the track God has laid out for you. Disregard those voices that tell you to give up on your dream—unless the voice is God's (1 Chronicles 28:3).

Take heart, and even though delays come your way, wait. Relax. God has everything under control. You're on His timeline. All is well.

Lord, thank You for making me a part of Your plan. I find peace in knowing You never hurry. So I pray You would help me to slow down, to walk in Your rhythm, to patiently wait, knowing the fulfillment of my dream is on Your timeline, not mine.

PRAYER JAR INSPIRATION:

Because God is never in a hurry, I can relax in Him.

OPEN EYES AND EARS

Your eyes shall see your Teacher. And your ears shall hear
a word behind you, saying, "This is the way, walk in it,"
when you turn to the right or when you turn to the left.

ISAIAH 30:20–21 ESV

Often in life, we will find ourselves at a crossroads, looking for guidance as to which way we should go. Thankfully, we need not make that choice alone. We can ask God for help. Yet we need to have not only our eyes open but our ears as well.

Author Donald Walsch wrote, "God is speaking to all of us all the time. The question is not, to whom does God talk? The question is, who listens?"

Are you listening? Are your ears open? Or are you too busy making up a list of pros and cons for each route and trusting in your own judgment and wisdom over God's? Or perhaps you are so blind and deaf that you don't even know you are at a crossroads. You are not open to God's *"Psssst! Daughter, there's an opportunity for you here!"*

Today, as you come before God in prayer, ask Him to open your eyes to His presence and your ears to His direction. Then walk where He wills.

Lord God, may my eyes be open to Your presence, my ears to Your
voice. What would You have me see? What would You have me hear?

PRAYER JAR INSPIRATION:

The Lord is my Guide.

THE BEST PATHWAY

You are my hiding place; you protect me from trouble. You surround me with songs of victory. The Lord says, "I will guide you along the best pathway for your life. I will advise you and watch over you."

PSALM 32:7–8 NLT

When you need a place to hide out until the dust settles, God is the ultimate hiding place for you. For in Him, you not only find refuge from trouble but are surrounded with songs and shouts of victory. There you can find a new direction from God, who is committed to leading you along the best road for your life here on earth.

Yes, God is here to give you all the advice you need. But you need to actually follow it. God doesn't want you to be like a stubborn mule that needs coaxing or goading or the horse that won't be led unless someone puts a bridle on it and pulls with all his might.

God promises that when you trust in Him and follow the plan He gives you, you'll be surrounded by unfailing love. So run to God. Bask in His songs of victory. Then listen to and follow His advice, trusting that He does indeed know best.

Thank You, Lord, for watching over me as I grow in trust and obedience.

PRAYER JAR INSPIRATION:

*I trust God's advice and guidance, for I know
He'll put me on the best pathway for my life.*

SPRINGING INTO LOVE

"Feed the hungry, and help those in trouble. Then your light will shine out from the darkness, and the darkness around you will be as bright as noon. The LORD will guide you continually, giving you water when you are dry and restoring your strength. You will be like a well-watered garden, like an ever-flowing spring."

ISAIAH 58:10–11 NLT

Feeling as if your life is a bit drab and dry? Are you finding yourself somewhat weak in your faith? Take God's advice, and revive your life by stepping out of your comfort zone to help someone else. When you do, you'll start glowing with the light of God's love. People will notice. And so will God.

When you walk in the ways of love, you can be sure God will be guiding you every moment. He'll give you water when you feel dry. He'll renew your strength when you feel weak. And before you know it, you'll be flourishing in God's garden.

I've been feeling a bit blah, Lord. Show me who I can help, what I might do to ease someone else's burdens. Lead me in the ways of love and caring as I shine Your light into someone else's life and become revived myself along the way.

PRAYER JAR INSPIRATION:

Guide me, Lord, as I spring into love, sharing Your light with others.

THE GOD WHO SEES YOU

*The angel of the L*ORD *found her by a spring of water in the wilderness,
the spring on the way to Shur. And he said, "Hagar, servant of
Sarai, where have you come from and where are you going?"*

Sometimes we get so confused we don't know whether we're coming or
going. That's what happened to Hagar, who had run away from Sarah.

God had promised the aging Sarah and Abraham a child. After
patiently waiting for years and still no baby, Sarah gave her maid
Hagar to Abraham, thinking they'd gain a child that way. Hagar *did*
get pregnant. But then she lorded it over Sarah. And when Sarah
began mistreating Hagar in return, the maid ran away.

Hagar hadn't even been looking for God's direction. But He'd
been keeping watch over her. So, God asked Hagar where she was
coming from and where she was going to. After Hagar admitted she
was running away from Sarah, God told her to go right back and
submit to Sarah's authority. Then He promised her a son.

Just as God saw Hagar, He sees you. And if you keep your ears
open, you can hear His directive. Your job is to follow it, even if that
means retracing your steps.

*"God Who Sees" (Genesis 16:13 HCSB) me no matter
where I am, lead where You would have me go.*

PRAYER JAR INSPIRATION:

Father God has His eyes on me. He will not let me stray.

WORD WAITING

I wait for Your word. My eyes fail [with longing, watching] for [the fulfillment of] Your promise. . . . You are my hiding place and my shield; I wait for Your word. . . . I rise before dawn and cry [in prayer] for help; I wait for Your word. . . . The unfolding of Your [glorious] words give light; their unfolding gives understanding to the simple (childlike).

PSALM 119:81–82, 114, 147, 130 AMP

When you need direction, you'll find it in God's Word. His Word is a lamp to your feet; it shines a light on your path (Psalm 119:105). But you'll never find His direction unless you seek it. And in that seeking, you must have patience. For you may have to do some waiting.

In the meantime, rest in God. Hide in Him. Allow Him to cover you completely. For while you're in hiding, He'll restore, strengthen, and renew your mind, spirit, and soul, readying you for the task ahead. Know that in God's good time, His Word will give you the light and understanding you need to follow His path.

Lord, thank You for allowing me to rest, hide, and renew myself in You as I await Your good Word—in Your time, not mine.

PRAYER JAR INSPIRATION:

I don't just hope but expect God's Word to shine a light on my path. His guidance will be worth waiting for!

WHERE YOUR STRENGTH LIES

The Lord God, the Holy One of Israel has said this,
"In returning [to Me] and rest you shall be saved,
in quietness and confident trust is your strength."

ISAIAH 30:15 AMP

It never works out well when God's people think they have a better plan than He.

Speaking through Isaiah, God told the people of Judah that sorrow awaited them because they made plans contrary to His and they made alliances that were not directed by His Spirit. Without consulting God, they went to Egypt for help, putting their trust in Pharaoh's protection instead of God's! God told them that doing so would only lead them to humiliation and disgrace.

Things were so bad that God's people not only refused to heed His instructions but also told His prophets, "Don't tell us what is right. Tell us nice things. Tell us lies. Forget all this gloom. Get off your narrow path. Stop telling us about your 'Holy One of Israel'" (Isaiah 30:10–11 NLT). Yikes!

Want to be on the right side of God? Follow His path; turn to Him for advice. Then you will find the rest and salvation you're seeking. And you'll find your strength by settling down and trusting in Him and His Spirit, completely depending on Him for your present and future.

I trust in You, Lord. Be my strength.

PRAYER JAR INSPIRATION:

You, Lord, are my hope, my confidence, my strength, my way.

FOREVER GUIDE

*I will bless the LORD who has counseled me; indeed, my heart (mind)
instructs me in the night. . . . Let me hear Your lovingkindness
in the morning, for I trust in You. Teach me the way in which
I should walk, for I lift up my soul to You. . . . This is God, our
God forever and ever; He will be our guide even until death.*

PSALM 16:7, 143:8, 48:14 AMP

Even while you're sleeping, God is guiding you through your dreams
and visions; the Divine touches your heart and mind. That's why some
mornings you wake up with an amazing idea, a new direction you
never before imagined, a way you can please or serve Him.

Other times, your night might be filled with trouble and distress,
leaving you to awaken discouraged. That's when you must open the
Good Book and read about the love and kindness God wants to pour
over you, over and over again. Knowing He holds a forever love for
you inspires you to trust Him not just to direct you but to teach you
the way you should go.

Take courage! God's guidance is available to you morning, noon,
and night. He will guide you even until death.

Guide me, Lord, in Your love and wisdom, day and night.

PRAYER JAR INSPIRATION:

God is my forever Guide on both sides of heaven.

187

THE LORD'S PRESENCE

*Whether it was two days or a month or a year that the cloud
[of the LORD's presence] lingered over the tabernacle, staying
above it, the Israelites remained camped and did not set out;
but when it was lifted, they set out. At the command of the LORD
they camped, and at the command of the LORD they journeyed on.*

NUMBERS 9:22–23 AMP

The cloud of God represented His presence among His people, a presence that was with them night and day. As long as the cloud lingered over the ark of God, the people stayed put. But when the cloud lifted, they set out, following wherever He led.

God's presence, His Spirit, continues on. By that Spirit, God continues to direct His people, instructing their hearts when they can rest and when He would have them move on.

Today, pray to Father God that He would direct you—that He would lead you where He would have you go. Pray that He would not allow your mind to have the final say but that His Spirit—the Companion He left with you to guide, comfort, and strengthen—would have the last word.

*Spirit of God, instruct my heart in the way You would have me
go. Give me patience if Your will and way are for me to rest;
and give me courage when You would have me set out.*

PRAYER JAR INSPIRATION:

*I hope in and follow the Divine Presence,
the Holy Spirit that directs my heart's way.*

HOPE
for Tomorrow

There are times when the future looks uncertain or even bleak, and we might be tempted to worry or give in to despair. Even in the most stressful or frightening moments, God is with us and offers hope for tomorrow. "Therefore do not worry about tomorrow, for tomorrow will worry about itself" (Matthew 6:34 NIV).

What a comfort it is to know that our hope relies not on the uncertainties of tomorrow but on the promises of God. When worry sets in, it should help if we remind ourselves to take one day at a time, for only God knows what the future holds. He is, and always will be, in complete control.

God has a plan for each of us, and He wants us to face the future with hope. "'For I know the plans I have for you,' declares the LORD, 'plans to prosper you and not to harm you, plans to give you hope and a future'" (Jeremiah 29:11 NIV).

Isn't it comforting to know that the heavenly Father has a plan for our lives and that we can face our tomorrows with hope?

YOUR FAITHFUL LORD

"I have loved you with an everlasting love; therefore with lovingkindness I have drawn you and continued My faithfulness to you."... "There is [confident] hope for your future," says the Lord.

JEREMIAH 31:3, 17 AMP

God has loved, is loving, and always will love you. His love for you is everlasting. And it's because He loves you that He has drawn you to Himself so that you can play your part in His plan and further His kingdom by loving and drawing others to His light.

God would have it that you need nothing more than His love to content you—that you need not desire anything more than Him to find true joy. All afflictions you face are temporary, all woes are passing, all fears are fleeting. When you keep this in mind, you will find peace in the present and have confident hope for your future.

Don't waste your time and energy on worry, fears, or angst. Instead, live in the present with the Lord whose love and hope for you will never ever end.

The fact that You will always love me touches something deep within me, Lord. Because of You and Your everlasting love, I am content and filled with joy.

PRAYER JAR INSPIRATION:

I am a woman confident of God's love and filled with hope for my future.

FAITH, LOVE, AND HOPE

*We have heard of your faith in Christ Jesus and your love for all
of God's people, which come from your confident hope of what
God has reserved for you in heaven. You have had this expectation
ever since you first heard the truth of the Good News.*

COLOSSIANS 1:4–5 NLT

Wouldn't it be great for others to hear about your faith and love, about the trust you have in Jesus, about your affection for all believers—all of which are born out of your hope of what God has reserved for you in heaven?

At this point you may be wondering, *What are those heavenly rewards awaiting me?* Someday you will be transformed. You'll see God's face, walk down streets paved with gold, and nevermore feel pain or sorrow. One day you'll reside forever after in the light of the Lord's presence! Knowing these rewards are in your future is what will surely help you get through whatever may be happening in the moment.

Allow that future hope to ignite and sustain your present faith in Jesus and to fire up your affectionate love for all believers. And you will find yourself and your world transformed.

*Help me, Lord, to focus on my future hope by building up my faith
in You and my love for others in the present. In Jesus' name, amen.*

PRAYER JAR INSPIRATION:

Faith, hope, and love are my present—and future—reward!

PRESSING ON

I do not consider that I have made it my own yet; but one thing I do: forgetting what lies behind and reaching forward to what lies ahead, I press on toward the goal to win the [heavenly] prize of the upward call of God in Christ Jesus.

PHILIPPIANS 3:13–14 AMP

At times we become so mired in our past that we become trapped in our woulda, coulda, shouldas. We're left unable to find a way to walk freely in our present or hold any sort of hope for the future. This is not a pleasant or productive place to be. Fortunately, the apostle Paul gave us tips on how we can get unstuck.

Although we may have a long way to go in our walk of faith, there's one mindset we can adopt to move forward. We can forget what lies behind us and reach for what lies ahead. Doing so allows us to press on in the present. It allows us to keep our eyes on Jesus, the One who stands on the water waiting for us to walk into His arms.

Today, do one thing: forget about the past and reach out for what lies ahead. With Jesus' help, your hope will spur you ever forward, taking you from treading water to swimming freestyle into your future.

Jesus, thank You for helping me forget what lies behind me and giving me the courage to reach forward.

PRAYER JAR INSPIRATION:

I'm reaching out for the hope that lies ahead of me!

ANCHORED HOPE

The king's command and law went into effect. . . . On the day when
the Jews' enemies had hoped to overpower them, just the opposite
happened. The Jews overpowered those who hated them.

ESTHER 9:1 HCSB

God wants your hope to rest in Him for your future, regardless of
how things may look in your present.

Consider Mordecai, an exiled Jew living in the Persian Empire. His
refusal to bow down to anyone other than his God enraged Haman,
an official of the king. So Haman convinced King Xerxes to sign an
edict stating that on a designated day all residents were to kill the
Jews living among them *and* plunder their goods. Haman then built
a gallows on which to hang Mordecai ahead of the slaughter.

But God worked things out so that Haman was hanged on his
own gallows. Then another edict was issued by the king allowing the
Jews to avenge themselves against their enemies. At the end of the
designated day, God reversed many fortunes in favor of His people.

No matter what trials are happening in your life, have a glad heart
and a tongue ready to shout praises to your Lord; allow your body to
rest in hope (Acts 2:26), knowing that God is the Master of turning
things around.

Today, Lord, my heart is merry and my mouth sings Your praises!

PRAYER JAR INSPIRATION:

My hope is forever anchored in God, the Master of turnarounds.

A WEANED CHILD

Lord, my heart is not proud; my eyes are not haughty. I don't concern myself with matters too great or too awesome for me to grasp. Instead, I have calmed and quieted myself, like a weaned child who no longer cries for its mother's milk. Yes, like a weaned child is my soul within me. O Israel, put your hope in the Lord—now and always.

Psalm 131:1–3 nlt

God's message to us stands in stark contrast to the message we get from the world. Our society would have us be proud, strong, and ambitious women, always finding a way to get ahead no matter who we might step on along the way.

Yet our God wants us to be humble. To trust not in our own strength and power but in His. To be satisfied with and grateful for what He has given us—no more, no less. To put all our hope in Him, now and always. For only then can we find true contentment and be able to calm and quiet our souls within us.

Today and every day, walk God's Way. And you will find rest for your body, spirit, and mind.

Because of You, Lord, I can find the peace and calm I crave.

PRAYER JAR INSPIRATION:

My hope rests in the Lord—now and always.

HANGING ON TO HOPE

"Look, God's home is now among his people! He will live with them,
and they will be his people. God himself will be with them. He will
wipe every tear from their eyes, and there will be no more death
or sorrow or crying or pain. All these things are gone forever."

REVELATION 21:3–4 NLT

The world can be a very harsh place. But those who trust in God, who
believe in Jesus, and who walk with His Spirit know a better place
lies ahead. And that place is heaven. There God will dwell among us.
He Himself, His very presence, will be with us. In His compassion,
our Father will gently wipe every tear from our eyes. No longer will
we cry, suffer death or pain, or feel anguish.

This is the world we hope for and look forward to. A new place,
a new home, a new life. The hope of that world is what will give us
grace to live through this one. Hang on to that hope.

I look forward to living in that new world with You,
Lord. To the hope of that world I cling.

PRAYER JAR INSPIRATION:

I live my life on earth with the hope of heaven in my heart.

THE SHEPHERD'S
ROD AND STAFF

Even though I walk through the [sunless] valley of the shadow
of death, I fear no evil, for You are with me; Your rod [to
protect] and Your staff [to guide], they comfort and console
me. . . . My cup overflows. Surely goodness and mercy and
unfailing love shall follow me all the days of my life.

PSALM 23:4–6 AMP

You need not live in fear or worry today or tomorrow. Because even though you may be walking in some hard places, the Lord is walking beside you. He's got His rod to fend off any evil that comes against you and His staff to make sure you keep on the right path.

Your life is filled with blessings—because you are the daughter of the Most High God. His goodness, mercy, and love will be with you not just all the days of your life on earth but throughout eternity.

So shake off any doubts and fears. The One with you is so much greater than any other thing above you, below you, or on the earth. He has encompassed you within His protective arm, ensuring that nothing can get to you without His say-so. And He'll make sure you stay on the right road—with His goodness, mercy, and love coming right behind.

Thank You, Lord, for keeping close to me through good times and bad.

PRAYER JAR INSPIRATION:

God's goodness and mercy are following me!

FIXED FOCUS

Our present troubles are small and won't last very long. Yet they produce for us a glory that vastly outweighs them and will last forever! So we don't look at the troubles we can see now; rather, we fix our gaze on things that cannot be seen. For the things we see now will soon be gone, but the things we cannot see will last forever.

2 CORINTHIANS 4:17–18 NLT

It's easy to get swallowed up by our trials and tribulations. But we need not go down that road at all. Even though our outer selves are continually wasting away, our inner selves are being renewed day by day. So these troubles we're passing through are miniscule, just little blips in the grand scheme of things. We can disregard them knowing good times are on their way and being prepared for us ahead of our arrival.

Today, look past your troubles. Fix your focus on the things that you cannot see. For they are what will be everlasting.

Lord, help me not to focus on all my troubles but to keep my eyes on the prize You have waiting for me at the end of this road.

PRAYER JAR INSPIRATION:

My focus is on God's goodness in the world to come!

NO WORRIES TODAY

"Do not worry or be anxious (perpetually uneasy, distracted), saying, 'What are we going to eat?' or 'What are we going to drink?' or 'What are we going to wear?' . . . But first and most importantly seek (aim at, strive after) His kingdom and His righteousness [His way of doing and being right—the attitude and character of God], and all these things will be given to you also."

MATTHEW 6:31, 33 AMP

It's exhausting trying to get through your day when your mind is focused on what you might need for tomorrow! That kind of fretting can only lead to stress.

Jesus has a better idea. Instead of worrying about what you will eat, drink, or wear tomorrow, seek out God—how He would have you live, what He would have you do today. Make Him your priority. . . because God knows exactly what you need and has you *more* than covered regarding the material side of things.

So, precious daughter of God, put aside your worries about tomorrow. Seek out your Father today, knowing He will never let you down.

Help me, Lord, to put aside any worries about tomorrow and to seek You and Your way of doing things today. In Jesus' name, amen.

PRAYER JAR INSPIRATION:

Undistracted by tomorrow's needs, I can focus on God today!